Signposts

How To Be a Catholic Man in the World Today

By
Bill Bawden and Tim Sullivan

theWORD
among us

The Word Among Us Press
9639 Doctor Perry Road
Ijamsville, Maryland 21754
www.wau.org

ISBN: 0-932085-38-5

Design by David Crosson

Imprimatur

It is a great joy to grant an *Imprimatur* to this study series, *Signposts: How To Be a Catholic Man in the World Today*. An imprimatur is an official statement of the local bishop that the text in question has been reviewed and contains nothing contrary to the teachings of the Church.

Signposts: How To Be a Catholic Man in the World Today is a very positive affirmation of Catholic teaching. In addition, it is a very practical guide enabling men of faith to live and practice the fullness of their Catholic faith. Therefore I not only grant an imprimatur but also highly recommend this series to all men of good will.

Most Reverend Eusebius J. Beltran
Archbishop of Oklahoma City
December 31, 1998

Acknowledgements

This series of lesson plans for Christian men is the result of collaboration, not just between the two authors, but with the many friends and colleagues whose gifts helped it to completion.

First, we are deeply grateful to Dr. Roy Forsythe, without whom the work would never have been conceived. Roy, who suggested that we develop a study guide for Catholic men because of the scarcity of available Catholic-oriented material, has been a constant source of encouragement as well as a wonderful critic.

We are also grateful to our immediate superiors, Bishop Edward J. Slattery and Father John A. Petuskey, for their encouragement and especially for allowing the time to develop the plans.

A number of other people have contributed to the finished product: Jim Doherty, for developing drafts on three of the lesson plans; David May, for his critique of a number of the lessons; Kay Janda, for proof reading; and Marsha Hoegger, for allowing us to draw on her computer expertise. We are also grateful to Kevin Lynch of the *Answer the Call* men's ministry in Cincinnati for his mentorship and encouragement; to Jeff Smith of *The Word Among Us* for having the faith in us and this work to publish it; and especially to Patty Mitchell for her enduring efforts and guiding hand in editing this plan.

We are indebted to a number of men whose names we don't even know who allowed us to use them as test groups for the study plan. They are members of the men's study groups at the Catholic Parish of St. John the Baptist, Edmond, Oklahoma, under the leadership of Dr. Roy Forsythe, and at Sts. Peter and Paul Parish, Cushing, Oklahoma, under the leadership of Jack Forsyth and Kenny Longbrake. Their critiques and suggestions were of great assistance in refining our ideas.

Finally, we thank the Most Reverend Eusebius J. Beltran, Archbishop of Oklahoma City, for his encouragement and for taking the time to review the document in order to issue his imprimatur.

Bill Bawden
Tim Sullivan

Introduction

I urge you therefore, brothers, by the mercies of God, to offer your bodies as a living sacrifice, holy and pleasing to God, your spiritual worship. Do not conform yourself to this age but be transformed by the renewal of your mind, that you may discern what is the will of God, what is good and pleasing and perfect. (Romans 12:1-2)

This quotation is obviously not from a modern textbook on how to be a real man, or from an article on "pop" male psychology. However, it does offer a challenge to the individual who is sincerely searching for an authentic Christian life.

It is confusing to be a man today, particularly a Christian man. There is a natural tension between the stereotypical male—the one many of us were taught to be, the male of the media—and the male that God calls men to be. Men are expected to play a variety of roles and to know how to bounce from one role to the other as the wind blows. The man of today is expected to be protective and hard working on the one hand, and gentle and supportive on the other. What is a man to do?

To further complicate matters, many sincere men are trying to reclaim aspects of their lives that in the past have been abdicated: spiritual leadership of the family; the ability to express love and emotion; and relationships with other men that don't have to flow from a mutual love for sports, work, or other "men stuff."

Signs of Hope

There is evidence of a spiritual renewal among men. Promise Keepers, a national men's organization, has issued a wake-up call through their stadium events for all Christian men to stand and be counted as godly men of integrity. Local and regional events such as Cincinnati's *Answer the Call*, Oklahoma City's *In the Father's Footsteps*, and New Orleans' *Catholic Men in Action* are providing a source of energy and rejuvenation to men's faith. Through the Holy Spirit, God is knocking at the door to our hearts.

There are many issues that men need to confront. It's a different ball game today. Men need help in sorting out all the new demands being made on them. How do we do that effectively, and at the same time, enjoy the process of getting there?

That's the reason for this series of lesson plans for small group discussions for men. *Signposts: How To Be a Catholic Man in the World Today* is not a scholarly Bible Study, but a series of lessons that are focused on issues of concern to men in the ordinariness of their everyday lives. Holy Scripture and various church documents are drawn upon to help clarify the issues.

Small Fellowship Groups for Men

What are small fellowship groups for men? They are gatherings of men, usually from the same parish, who get together to discuss their lives in the light of their Catholic faith and to share their faith and experiences through friendship, prayer, and fraternity.

Most groups generally meet for ninety minutes to pray, socialize, discuss their faith and the issues they are grappling with in their lives. They support, affirm, and share insights about the difficulties men encounter in both their home and work lives. They also seek God's help in dealing with the issues they confront every day. Members strive to reinforce Christian values in their home, reach out to share those values with others in their group, and support other men who are struggling to do the same.

Most men who have attended a small discussion group quickly discover the benefits they offer. Men participating in such groups cultivate friendships among their fellow parishioners, have fun, and learn from one another how to be a better husband, father, son, employee, and Catholic parishioner. Many men say they have grown by this experience, which has helped them to form stronger and happier families and to cope better with the stresses they encounter at work.

How to Use the Plan

A strong facilitator is of great value in using these lesson plans. He need not be an expert in scripture or church doctrine, although some knowledge of both will be helpful. The facilitator does not function as a teacher. His primary responsibilities are to keep the group focused on the particular subject, to see that each man in the group has an opportunity to participate, and to keep the group discussions moving.

If the group is newly organized, we suggest that one person serve as facilitator. After the group has bonded and the men have become comfortable with each other, the facilitator's role may be rotated among the men who are interested in leading the discussions. This will prepare men to lead another group when the current group grows beyond eight or ten men.

Signposts: How To Be a Catholic Man in the World Today has been designed to provide a flexible resource for small groups of men. The following format is suggested, but each group should adapt it to be comfortable and workable for its group.

Music: This can be a recording or a shared song. Some groups may prefer not to start with music.

Opening Prayer: The prayer can be a brief prayer service planned by one of the men, a spontaneous prayer, or any form suitable to the group. The format doesn't matter as long as it is heartfelt and the meeting is started with prayer.

Accountability*:* One of the values of belonging to a small group of men is that the men in the group can support each other in their quest for living a Christian life (Proverbs 27:17). At the end of each lesson plan, each man is encouraged to develop a plan of action for the coming week to address some area of weakness or some area that needs to be improved in his life. After the group prays together, it is suggested that a few minutes be devoted to sharing how well each man did with his plan for the previous week. When some of the men are struggling with an issue, they may want to ask for the prayers of the group.

Lesson Plan*:* The lesson plans are designed to be covered in a one-hour session. Depending on the interaction of the group, how well the participants have prepared, or the amount of time spent in sharing and prayer, any lesson could take longer. The group may decide if it wants to eliminate any of the questions, or if it wants to extend the lesson into the following session.

Concluding Prayer: The meetings should always be closed with a prayer in which the participants may lift up their own needs. This would be a good time to pray for any of the men who need God's grace in an area.

Suggestions:

- Form teams of two who will call each other during the week to encourage one another.

- Using multiple translations of the Bible can sometimes be confusing. Discuss the desirability of using a standard Catholic translation such as the *New American Bible*.

- The individual lesson plans are grouped by general topic. However, it is not necessary to strictly follow that format if another format works better for the group. The lesson plans are meant to be a springboard for group discussion on a particular topic and not a rigid format to be precisely followed.

- Encourage personal witnessing and "testimonies" to build faith among the men.

- While a predictable and comfortable format is helpful, flexibility is also necessary at times to adjust to an individual's needs.

- Start with a few moments of socializing and stop on time.

- Be ready to welcome new members to the group, and to break up into two groups if the original group grows too large.

It is our prayer that each person using this series will be strengthened in his faith, in his role as husband and father, and as a disciple of our Lord Jesus.

But you, remain faithful to what you have learned and believed, because you know from whom you learned it, and that from infancy you have known [the] sacred scriptures, which are capable of giving you wisdom for salvation through faith in Christ Jesus. (2 Timothy 3:14-15)

Deacon Bill Bawden, Pastoral Associate
The Catholic Parish of St. John the Baptist
Edmond, Oklahoma

Deacon Tim Sullivan, Executive Director
Catholic Charities
Diocese of Tulsa, Oklahoma

Table of Contents

Man and God

Lesson 1

Searching for the Living God

Exodus 3:1-14; Psalm 19; John 14:8-14

Catechism: 28; 205-206; 222-227

Dan had been raised Catholic. He went to Catholic schools from kindergarten through college, although it was only upon the birth of his first child that he began to take his faith seriously. He became active in his parish, eventually becoming head of the parish council. To all who knew him, he was successful in both his professional and religious life. One summer, Dan and his wife went on a spiritual retreat, not so much to get closer to God as to just have some time together. One night during the retreat, they attended a reconciliation service. As Dan listened to the homily that night, a strange thing happened. He had an intense experience of God's loving presence; his whole body tingled from his head to his toes as God penetrated every fiber of Dan's being.

Dan realized that, despite his outwardly religious behavior, he had never felt himself worthy of God's love. He had never prayed with the expectation that God was real, that he was alive and active, and that he had intervened and would continue to do so in Dan's life. Dan now realized that God was always walking with him and communicating his presence to him in many, many ways.

1. In what ways in your daily life is the presence of God made manifest to you?

_____

_____

_____

_____

_____

2. Describe a time, or times, in your life when God's presence seemed to elude you. How did you feel?

_____

_____

_____

_____

_____

3. In what ways can we come to know the living God?

_____

_____

_____

_____

_____

4. Based on paragraphs 222-227 of the Catechism, discuss the consequences in your life of coming to know the living God.

_____

_____

_____

_____

_____

5. What is the biggest obstacle that you have encountered in your search for God?

_____

_____

_____

_____

_____

6. Describe the false gods that you have created, or followed, in your life.

_____

_____

_____

_____

_____

7. How well does your life give witness to the living God in you?

_____

_____

_____

_____

_____

Action Plan:

Over the next week, I will be more consistently aware of God's presence in my life by:
- looking for God's presence in the ordinariness of my life.
- imagining myself as watching Moses and the burning bush and reflecting on my feelings.
- spending a few minutes each day looking for evidence of God in my life.
- other:

_____

_____

_____

Lesson 2

Our Relationship with Jesus

John 5:19-24, 6:35-40, 10:25-30; Ephesians 2:19-21; Colossians 1:15-20
Catechism: 161; 425; 448-450; 669

Matt had been listening to his friend Joe pour out his heart for over thirty minutes. While he seemed "together" on the surface, in his heart Joe felt lonely, aimless, and confused. Finally, Joe paused, looked at him and blurted out, "What should I do?" Matt knew that he should invite his friend to surrender his life more fully to Jesus. He hesitated, then responded, "I think you should recommit your life to Jesus." His friend asked, "How do I do that?" Matt found himself saying, "I don't know, but let's pray." Matt began, "Jesus, Joe wants you to be the Lord of his life. He gives his life completely to you from this day on. Help him to know you better and to love you and serve you. You are the Lord. You are his Savior. You are his King. Help him to know your will and follow it always."

1. Describe your relationship with Jesus.

_____

_____

_____

_____

_____

2. In what ways have you given your life to Jesus? In what ways are you holding back from him?

_____

_____

_____

_____

_____

3. How can you come to know Jesus more deeply?

_____

_____

_____

_____

_____

4. Identify the personal qualities of Jesus that seem most appealing to you.

_____

_____

_____

_____

5. Describe the relationship between Jesus and God the Father.

_____

_____

_____

_____

_____

6. How can you relate to your Father in heaven as Jesus related to him during his earthly ministry?

_____

_____

_____

_____

7. How does Jesus' love manifest itself in your life?

_____

_____

_____

_____

_____

Action Plan:

Over the next week, I will examine my relationship with Jesus by:
- reading one of the Gospels and imagining being with Jesus during his earthly ministry.
- asking Jesus to come into my heart in a deeper way.
- surrendering everything in my life over to him.
- other:

_____

_____

_____

Lesson 3

Prayer

Psalm 25; Luke 18:9-14; Matthew 6:5-13; Romans 8:26-27
Catechism: 2559-2565

It was Monday morning, and as he drove to his first appointment, John was pondering the homily he had heard at Mass the previous day. The one statement that stuck in his mind was when the priest said, "Prayer does not change God. Prayer changes people." John thought, "What could he have meant by that? Can prayer actually change a person's bad habits, or inspire him to serve God? Can we change the course of events in our lives through prayer? Can we alter God's will? Do I even know how to pray?"

1. Reflecting on the readings from the Catechism (2559-2565), how would you define prayer? How does this fit with your own personal concept of prayer?

   _____

   _____

   _____

   _____

   _____

2. Contrast praying from the heart to praying from the mind. Why are both important? Give an example of "prayer from the heart" in your own life.

   _____

   _____

   _____

   _____

   _____

3. Why do you think it is important to set aside time each day to devote to prayer? In what ways would this deepen your relationship with the Lord?

   _____

   _____

   _____

   _____

4. In the Parable of the Pharisee and the Tax Collector (Luke 18:9-14), why do you think that humility in prayer was so pleasing to God? Why is humility important for you today?

_____

_____

_____

_____

_____

5. How do you prepare yourself to come into the presence of the Lord? What specific things could you do to make your prayer more fruitful?

_____

_____

_____

_____

_____

_____

6. Describe a recent time when your prayer life was dry. Why do you think this was so?

_____

_____

_____

_____

_____

7. Share with the group a time when you feel God answered one of your prayers. What makes you feel that the prayer was answered?

_____

_____

_____

_____

_____

Action Plan:

Over the next week, I will pay more attention to my prayer life by:
- scheduling a specific time each day for prayer.
- spending a few minutes each day reflecting on my prayer habits and how they impact my life.
- praying each day for my family.
- other:

_____

_____

_____

A Simple Guide to Prayer

Choose a Time and Place.
Make it a specific time dedicated only to prayer—a time when you are alert and clear. (Psalm 92:1-2)
Make sure it's a place where you are free from distraction and interruption. (Matthew 6:6)

Lay Aside All Other Concerns.
Examine your conscience and repent of your sins. (Psalm 130)
Let God's mercy cleanse your conscience. (Romans 8:1-2)
Put aside anxieties, problems, and struggles. (Hebrews 12:1-2)

Open Your Heart to the Gospel.
Consciously say "Yes" to these truths each day:
- God created me out of love and loves me always. (1 John 4:10)
- God sent Jesus to give us life. (John 3:16)
- By his death and resurrection, Jesus conquered sin and death. (John 5:24)
- Jesus promised to be with us and to send the Holy Spirit. (John 14:15-16,23)
- Jesus intercedes for us in heaven. (Hebrews 7:25)
- Jesus is coming again. (Matthew 16:27)

Praise God.
Express your love and gratitude to your heavenly Father, to his Son Jesus, and to the Holy Spirit. (Psalms 95; 136; Hebrews 13:15; 1 Peter 2:9)
Worship God honestly and from your heart. (Matthew 6:7-8)

Dwell in the Presence of God.
Listen actively to God in your heart as your read scripture. (Isaiah 66:2)
Sit quietly in God's presence and let his love touch your heart. (Psalm 131)

Intercede with Faith and Trust.
Pray for the world, for the church, for your family, your friends, and yourself. (Matthew 7:7-11)

Write in Your Journal.
What has God said to you?
What do you want to carry into the day to keep your mind fixed on Jesus?
What petitions will you keep close to your heart?

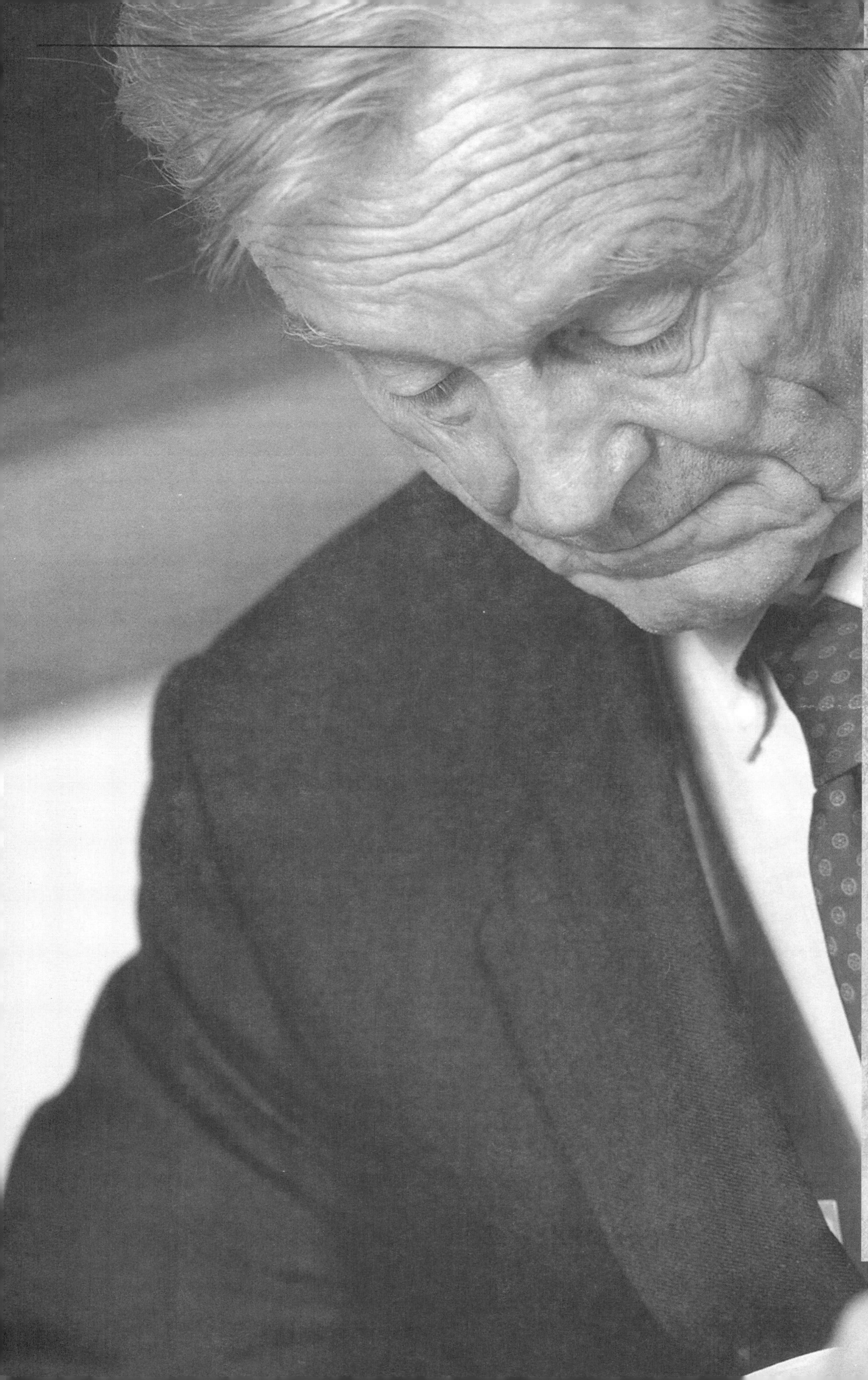

A Simple Guide to Prayer

17

Lesson 4

Seek First the Kingdom

Our Dependence on God

Luke 12:22-34; Mark 10:46-52; 2 Corinthians 9:6-10
Catechism: 302-305

Jeff was two payments behind on his mortgage. A close friend, who acted as his financial advisor, had just called to ask Jeff if he had enough money to make the payments. Jeff told him no. Frustrated, he went to get the mail. In the mail was an envelope from a person unknown to him. Inside the envelope was a check, totally unsolicited, from a stranger who had somehow learned of the tough times Jeff and his family were having. The check would just cover the amount due on the mortgage.

Jeff began to cry. He knew he was the beneficiary of some special attention from God, and was grateful. He knew God's action in his life would help him to trust in God's providence in the future.

1. Describe a situation in your own life (financial, family, or work) when things looked bleak and God provided the support that was needed.

_____
_____
_____
_____
_____

2. Read Mark 10:46-52. How likely are you, like Bartimaeus, to cry out to God when you are in need? Why was Bartimaeus' request so pleasing to Jesus?

_____
_____
_____
_____
_____

3. Jesus said to seek first the kingdom of God and everything we need will be given to us (Luke 12:31). What's your first reaction to this statement?

_____
_____
_____
_____

4. Do you put God first in your life, before everything else? Explain your answer.

_____

_____

_____

_____

5. Describe yourself in terms of how much control you like to have over the details of your life.

_____

_____

_____

_____

6. Describe in your own life the areas in which you are confident and the areas in which you have fears and anxieties.

_____

_____

_____

_____

_____

7. How would you respond to the suggestion that everything that happens to you, good or bad, is a gift?

_____

_____

_____

_____

_____

Action Plan:

Over the next week, I will examine my dependence on God by:
- turning to God first when I am in need.
- making a list of all that I believe is a gift from God.
- remembering when something didn't work out because I had the attitude, "I'll do it my way."
- other:

_____

_____

_____

I Have Called You by Name: You Are Mine
Lesson 5

God's Unconditional Love

Isaiah 43:1-2; 1 John 4:7-21; Romans 8:12-17
Catechism: 1; 2782-2785

After Mass one Sunday, Andy took his family to the river for a picnic and some swimming. As they were relaxing, Andy heard a cry from his fifteen-year-old son. He had caught his foot in some brush beneath the water and couldn't break free; the current of the water had begun to pull him under. Andy ran to the river, jumped in and freed his son, who was able to climb up on the river bank. The current swept over Andy, and he was carried under the water, and down the river. His body was found the next day, two miles downstream.

1. Try to put yourself inside Andy's head as he heard his son's cry for help. What do you imagine must have been his thoughts? How do you think you would react in a similar situation?

_____
_____
_____
_____
_____

2. God sacrificed his son Jesus out of love for us. Share with each other how you feel about this offering of love after discussing Andy's giving of his life for his son.

_____
_____
_____
_____
_____

3. Why did God create you? How are you called to respond?

_____
_____
_____
_____

4. In Isaiah 43:1, God says, "I have called you by name: you are mine." What does it mean to you for God to claim you as his own?

_____

_____

_____

_____

5. Discuss what it means to you to be invited to be God's adopted son (See Romans 8:12-17).

_____

_____

_____

_____

6. How do we come to know and believe the love God has for us? Share some of the ways that you see God's love manifested to you.

_____

_____

_____

_____

_____

7. What are the things in your life that keep you from knowing and believing that God loves you unconditionally?

_____

_____

_____

_____

Action Plan:

Over the next week, I will look for the manifestations of God's love in my life by:
- asking God the Father to reveal his deep love for me, just like a father has for his son.
- spending time each day reflecting on where I encountered God.
- trying to be more aware of the reflection of God in the people I meet.
- other:

_____

_____

Lesson 6

Conversion

Mark 16:15-16; Luke 22:47-62; John 21:15-17; Acts 1:16-18
Catechism 1427-1429

Mike had known Roy for a number of years—both worked for the same firm—but they had never spent much time together until they attended the same conference. Driving together to the convention city together, they shared about their families, their hobbies, and their ambitions. As they became comfortable with one another, the conversation shifted to religion. Mike revealed that he had experienced a conversion at a weekend retreat the year before. He told Roy that since that weekend, he felt like a new man, reborn in Christ. Now, each day, he felt called to continue this conversion process by staying close to God through prayer and the sacraments. Mike's excitement and enthusiasm made Roy begin to desire a renewal of his own faith.

1. What disposition of the heart do you think is necessary for the kind of conversion that Mike experienced?

_____

_____

_____

_____

_____

2. The Catechism speaks of two conversions. If baptism is a "the first and fundamental conversion" (1427), why is the second conversion necessary?

_____

_____

_____

_____

_____

3. In the Scripture readings from Luke, John, and Acts, we hear of Peter and Judas betraying Jesus, and what eventually happened to each of them. Using the facts from the readings and your imagination, how would you tell the conversion story of each of these two men?

_____

_____

_____

_____

4. What relationship is there between conversion and repentance?

_____

_____

_____

_____

_____

5. How can frequent reception of the Sacraments of Reconciliation and the Eucharist help you in this process?

_____

_____

_____

_____

_____

_____

6. After reflecting on the significant events in your faith life, how would you tell your conversion story to another person?

_____

_____

_____

_____

_____

_____

7. Reflecting again on the story of Peter in Luke 22, what should be the results of your continuing conversion in your daily life?

_____

_____

_____

_____

_____

_____

Action Plan:

Over the next week, I will be more aware of my continuing conversion process by:
- writing about the significant conversion experiences in my life.
- sharing my conversion story with another person.
- trying to identify ongoing conversion experiences in my life.
- other:

_____

_____

Lesson 7

Our Inclination toward Sin

John 3:16-21; Romans 6:16-23; Ephesians 6:11-17; 1 Peter 2:24-25

Catechism: 391; 395; 1849-1850; 1868

Adam hadn't been to confession in years. His parents had encouraged him to make a spiritual retreat. Solely to appease them, he agreed. While on the retreat, Adam met a very special priest and decided to make a confession. As he disclosed his problems, including significant drug use, the priest laid a crucifix on Adam's shoulder and prayed intensely.

Adam had the sensation of an evil presence leaving his body. When the negative presence was gone, Adam's whole body felt warmed by a new, joyous sensation. It was as if every fiber of his being was now occupied by God.

Adam was transformed by this experience. Upon returning home from the retreat, he found that he had a new sensitivity to good and evil, and a greater ability to stay away from drugs. He could see how everything led either to light or to darkness.

1. In the above story, Adam recognized that he was a sinner because of specific sinful acts. Discuss your understanding of what it means to be "a sinner."

_____

_____

_____

_____

_____

2. Even if you are living a good life, how do St. Paul's comments about slavery apply to your life? What are the implications of being a slave to anyone or anything?

_____

_____

_____

_____

_____

3. Some people are uncomfortable with the idea of the existence of an evil spirit that can influence us. Based on the suggested readings, do you think Satan (the devil, the evil spirit, etc.) is real, and if so, how does he tempt you?

_____

_____

_____

_____

4. What process do you use to determine the presence and extent of sin in your life?

_____

_____

_____

_____

_____

5. St. Alphonsus Liguori (1696-1787) believed that through prayer, people could receive the grace they needed to overcome temptation. How can prayer help to keep you from sinning?

_____

_____

_____

_____

_____

_____

6. The Church provides the Sacrament of Reconciliation for forgiveness and absolution of sins. What fruits does this sacrament bear in your life?

_____

_____

_____

_____

_____

7. Reflecting on the passage from 1 Peter, explain what Jesus accomplished on the cross for us.

_____

_____

_____

_____

_____

Action Plan:

Over the next week, I will try to be more conscious on a regular basis of my own sins by:
- performing a daily examination of conscience and asking for God's grace in freeing me from the sin patterns in my life.
- setting a time to participate in the Sacrament of Reconciliation.
- other:

_____

_____

_____

An Examination of Conscience

The questions below are meant to help you prepare for the Sacrament of Reconciliation. As you pray over them, ask the Holy Spirit to bring to light areas in your life that need forgiveness—attitudes, habits, and relationships that keep you separated from God and cloud your relationship with his people. When you bring your needs to your heavenly Father in Confession, allow him not only to forgive you, but to change your heart. Remember: Nothing at all can separate you from his love.

1. Do I recognize God' authority over my life, or do I follow my own agenda? Is my life controlled by own ambitions or desires, my career, or a need for human respect, rather than God's word?

2. Can I see the envy, anger, lust, or hatred that keep me isolated from those who love me?

3. Are there relationships in my life that are marred, or even broken, by a lack of forgiveness? Have I allowed bitterness and resentment to keep me from forgiving anyone who has hurt me?

4. Are there any ways in which I am resisting God's invitation to let Jesus be born more fully in my life? Ways in which I am avoiding the call to decrease so that Jesus can increase?

5. Do I recognize the pride, self-righteousness, and complacency that keep me from coming before God and receiving his healing touch?

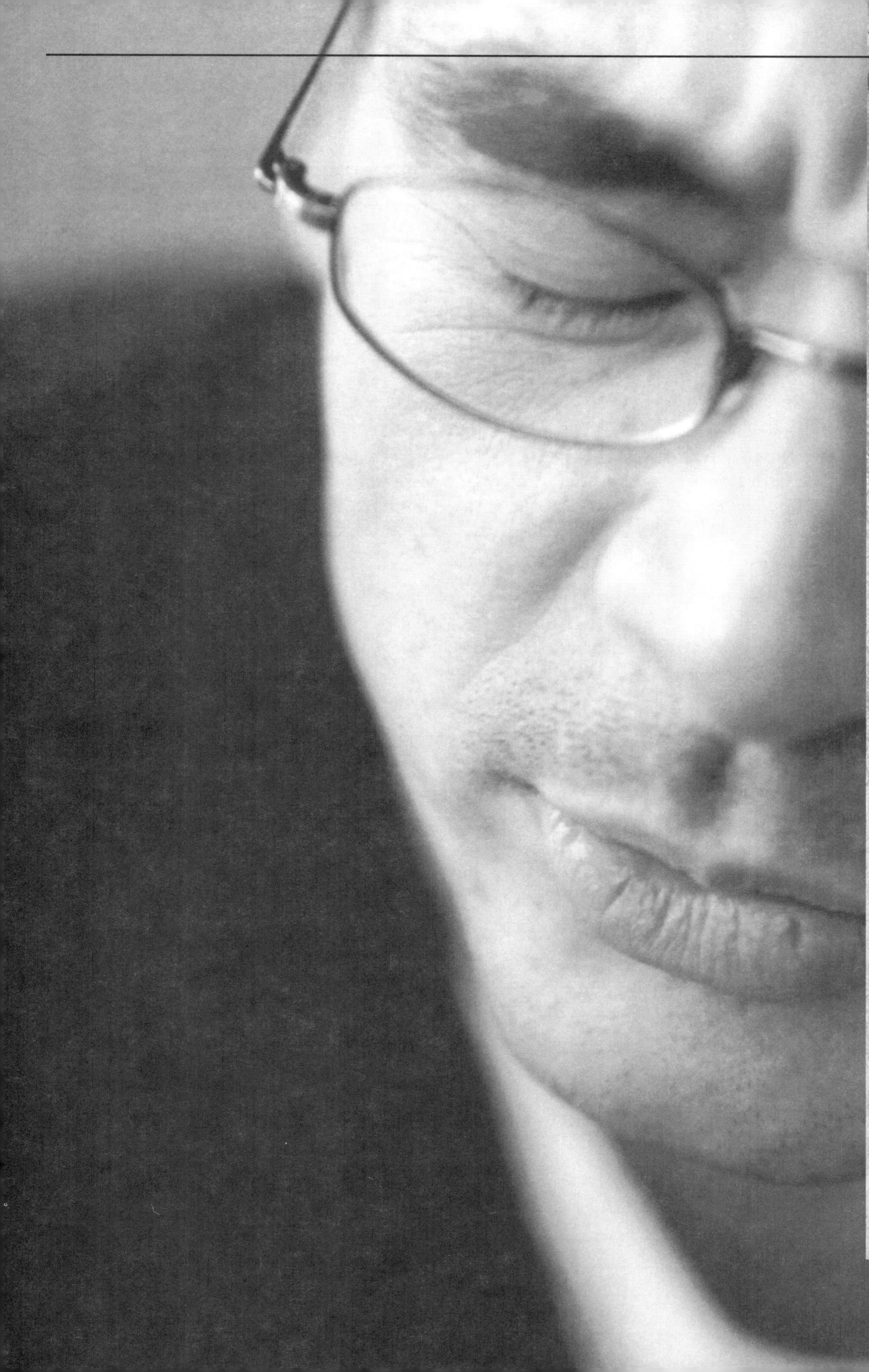

An Examination of Conscience

27

Lesson 8

Receiving the Holy Spirit

John 16:7-15; Acts 2:1-13; 1 Corinthians 12:4-11
Catechism: 683-686; 696; 1831-1832

Joe's aunt and uncle were about to celebrate their fiftieth wedding anniversary. They had expressly asked that no one bring gifts to the celebration. Joe sensed that there was something special he could do in honor of the occasion. He sat down at the computer and began to type. Within a short time, he had composed a very special prayer praising God for the wonderful qualities of his aunt and uncle and their life of faith together. When the prayer was read at the anniversary party, it brought tears to the eyes of many who were present.

What amazed Joe was that the writing of the prayer was unlike anything he had ever done before, and the words that came to him were not words he would normally use. In fact, the prayer had come so easily he didn't even think of himself as its author. "Maybe," Joe thought to himself, "this is how the Holy Spirit works."

1. Describe one event in which you sensed or experienced the presence and power of the Holy Spirit.

_____
_____
_____
_____
_____

2. Have you ever asked the Holy Spirit to come into your life in a more powerful way? If so, what happened after you prayed for this?

_____
_____
_____
_____
_____

3. In John 16:8, Jesus tells the apostles that when the Holy Spirit comes, he will "convict the world in regard to sin." In what ways might the Holy Spirit want to reveal your own sinfulness?

_____
_____
_____
_____
_____

4. Which gifts and fruits of the Holy Spirit has the Lord given to you? Which are the gifts and fruits you are most lacking? Which gifts and fruits do you most desire?

_____

_____

_____

_____

_____

5. There are references in the Bible to visible manifestations of the Holy Spirit, such as speaking in tongues and healing. Are you open to receiving these manifestations in your own life? Why or why not?

_____

_____

_____

_____

_____

6. The Holy Spirit is sometimes described in terms of fire (Acts 2:3 and Catechism 696, for example). Is there fire in your life? Why or why not?

_____

_____

_____

_____

_____

7. Describe what you think the Holy Spirit is doing these days to build up the Body of Christ.

_____

_____

_____

_____

_____

Action Plan:

Over the next week, I will be more open to the action of the Holy Spirit by:
- looking for God's actions in my own life though meditation, reflection, listening and reading God's word.
- looking for signs of the movement of the Holy Spirit in the lives of others.
- praying for the Lord to send the Holy Spirit to guide my life.
- other:

_____

_____

Lesson 9

The Eucharist

Luke 22:14-20; John 6:29-36,48-58; 1 Corinthians 11:23-27
Catechism: 1322-1327; 1373-1374

Bob was going through a difficult time. Personnel changes at work made it likely that he would lose his job. At home, his teenager's rebellious attitudes and actions were affecting everyone in the family. As Bob prayed for guidance, he felt more and more drawn to the Eucharist and began attending Mass each morning before work. Receiving Jesus each day gave him the strength and grace he needed to cope. The peace that he felt after taking Communion made it well worth the sacrifice of getting up early to get to Mass. Even when his schedule changed and he couldn't get to Mass every day, Bob eagerly looked forward to those times when he could receive Jesus in the Eucharist.

1. Why do you think Jesus left the Church with the gift of his Body and Blood? What do you think he intends for us through the Eucharist?

2. If you knew Jesus was going to be a guest in your home next week, how would you prepare?

3. Share a situation in which Jesus in the Eucharist has ministered personally to you.

4. What is meant by the "real presence of Jesus in the consecrated host"? (see Catechism 1374) How is this different from his presence in other ways, such as in scripture or in other people?

30

5. How can we prepare our hearts each time we receive Holy Communion?

_____

_____

_____

_____

_____

6. Jesus said, "Whoever eats my flesh and drinks my blood remains in me and I in him" (John 6:56). How does Christ abiding in us through the Eucharist help us to mature spiritually?

_____

_____

_____

_____

_____

7. Why do you think the Eucharist is "the source and summit of the Christian life" (Catechism 1324)? How can you make it more central to your own life in Christ?

_____

_____

_____

_____

_____

_____

Action Plan:

In order to develop a better understanding of the Eucharist, over the next week I will:
- read John 6 several times and pray over it.
- attend daily Mass at least once a week and, if possible, more frequently.
- pray over the readings for each Mass before I attend the celebration.
- pray that the Lord will bless me with the wisdom to experience the presence of Jesus in the Eucharist.
- other:

_____

_____

_____

A Guide to Preparing for Mass

If possible, try to get to church ten or fifteen minutes before Mass starts to prepare your heart for all that God intends to pour upon you during the liturgy. Take some time to ponder the following questions and to settle your heart in God's presence:

1. Do I have a sense of expectancy that God is inviting me to a banquet when I come to Mass?

2. What are my motivations for coming to Mass? Do I come out of a sense of duty? Or can I see Mass as an opportunity to spend time with the Lord?

3. What thoughts or attitudes keep me from lifting up my heart to God during Mass? Do I recognize the spiritual battle in which the evil one wants to rob me of my sense of God's presence?

4. Am I ready—to the best of my ability—to worship the Lord with my whole heart during Mass?

5. Do I have a sense that the whole family of God is coming to worship and rejoice in God's presence?

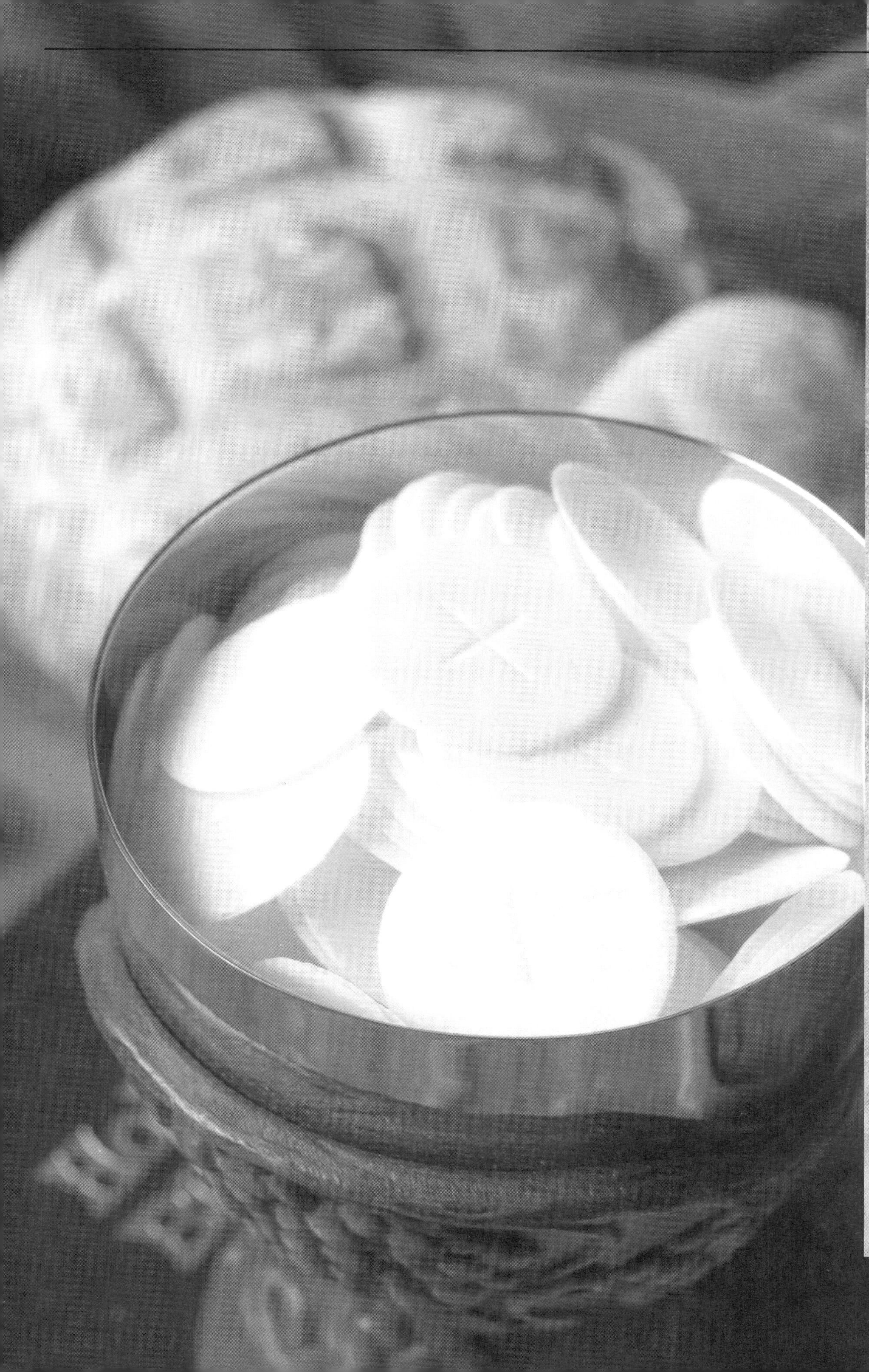

A Guide to Preparing for Mass

Lesson 10

Our Uniqueness Before God

Psalm 139:1-16; Matthew 10:29-31; 1 Corinthians 12:4-18

Catechism: 356-358

Like most men, John had spent his early adult years building a life for himself and his family. He was very goal-oriented and focused, and through diligence and hard work, he had acquired a decent income and a nice home. He was well regarded by all who knew him.

When the gag cards and gifts from his 40th birthday had faded from his memory, however, John began to get restless. He had always thought of himself as in control. Now he realized that he could not keep himself from getting older. He began to think about why he was created in the first place. He wondered whether his life would make a real difference.

1. What are the distinctive qualities of your life that show that God has created you for a unique purpose?

_____

_____

_____

_____

_____

2. How do these unique qualities provide you with the capacity to "make a difference"?

_____

_____

_____

_____

_____

3. Reflecting on paragraphs 356-358 of the Catechism, why do you think God created you?

_____

_____

_____

_____

_____

4. How are you called to share in God's life while living in this world?

_____

_____

_____

_____

_____

5. After reading Psalm 139, what aspects of your life make you want to hide from God?

_____

_____

_____

_____

_____

6. Reflect on the fact that Jesus died for you personally, for you individually. Share your response with the group.

_____

_____

_____

_____

_____

7. Upon your death, what words would you want to be placed on your gravestone?

_____

_____

_____

_____

_____

Action Plan:

Over the next week, I will try to be more conscious of God's active presence in my life by:
- spending time before the Blessed Sacrament meditating on my experience of God.
- creating a journal of my experience of God.
- pausing at least once each day and asking how I have experienced God in my life that day.
- working at letting go of my need to be in control.
- other:

_____

_____

_____

_____

Lesson 11

Doing versus Being

Matthew 6:33-34; 1 Thessalonians 5:16-18

Catechism: 2697-2699

Bill was having a spiritual crisis. In just a few months he was scheduled to be ordained as a permanent deacon, and he felt a real absence of God in his life. How could he serve other people as a spiritual leader when he himself did not have an intimate relationship with God? That really disturbed him. Bill attended Mass regularly and prayed from the Liturgy of the Hours each day. He worked full-time for his parish as a Pastoral Associate and was busily involved in ministry and corporal works of mercy. What was missing?

It took a quiet day of reflection for Bill to realize that he had become so busy *doing* that he had lost his sense of *being*, that place in one's life where God dwells. He had stopped praying and spending time with God. He still said his prayers, but he had become so wrapped up in the business of his ministry that he had basically stopped praying. He had stopped spending time just being with God.

1. How would you describe what it means "to be" in the presence of God?

   _____

   _____

   _____

   _____

   _____

2. What are the activities in your life that keep you busy *doing*, and how do these activities either enhance, or detract, from your sense of *being*?

   _____

   _____

   _____

   _____

   _____

3. From what part of your life do you derive the greatest fulfillment and satisfaction? How does this correlate with the admonition in Matthew 6:33 to seek first the kingdom of God and his righteousness?

   _____

   _____

   _____

   _____

4. Describe a specific time or incident in your life when you really experienced dwelling in the presence of the Lord (see Catechism 2699). How did you respond?

_____
_____
_____
_____
_____

5. How would you say your current prayer practices contribute to, or detract from, your sense of being in the presence of the Lord?

_____
_____
_____
_____
_____
_____

6. Describe a dark time when you felt God was not present to you. What do you think caused you to feel that way?

_____
_____
_____
_____
_____
_____

7. In your spiritual life, what are some of the high points and low points, and what themes, or cycles, seem to repeat themselves?

_____
_____
_____
_____
_____

Action Plan:

During the coming week I will work on my ability to find myself in the presence of God and to be able to just "be" by:
- not filling every moment of my day with productive or fun activities.
- avoiding television or radio for at least one day and spending that time quietly with the Lord.
- other:

_____
_____
_____

Lesson 12

God Can Speak to Me!

Listening to God

Acts 9:10-19; 2 Corinthians 12:8-9

Catechism: 2725-2745

Miguel and Maria had an important decision to make. Miguel had been offered a better job in another city. Taking the job seemed like a good career decision and would mean more money. But Miguel and Maria didn't want to jump at the opportunity without praying about it beforehand. The move would mean uprooting themselves and their children. Miguel and Maria took some time out of their schedules to pray before the Blessed Sacrament at their parish. They agreed to tell each other what they thought they should do only after they had both prayed. When they came together again, they were surprised. Both had received a strong sense that God wanted them to stay where they were. Miguel turned down the job offer, and several weeks later his company gave him an unexpected promotion. Both Miguel and Maria felt the promotion was a confirmation of what God had told them in prayer.

1. Have you ever sought the Lord in prayer about a decision you needed to make, or for wisdom about a situation that you were facing? How did he give you guidance? What did he say to you?

   _____
   _____
   _____
   _____
   _____

2. What does Miguel's and Maria's decision to seek God's wisdom say about their relationship with him and their priorities?

   _____
   _____
   _____
   _____
   _____

3. In 2 Corinthians 12, St. Paul beseeches the Lord to take away the "thorn" in his flesh. How do you think the Lord's answer helped St. Paul to endure his hardship?

   _____
   _____
   _____
   _____

4. Do you think Ananias (Acts 9) was surprised by what God had told him? How did Ananias' obedience to God's word bear fruit for the gospel?

_____
_____
_____
_____
_____

5. Do you believe God could speak to you in the same way he spoke to Ananias, St. Paul, or Miguel and Maria? Why or why not?

_____
_____
_____
_____
_____

6. Describe some ways in which you have coped with "dry times" in prayer, when you are not able to hear the Lord speaking to you.

_____
_____
_____
_____
_____

7. The Catechism speaks of a lack of faith as a hidden temptation in prayer (2732). How can a lack of faith prevent us from hearing what God wants to say to us?

_____
_____
_____
_____
_____

Action Plan:

Over the next week, I will try to listen to the Lord more often by:
- seeking God's wisdom in areas of my life where I am struggling.
- spending time each day quieting my mind and "listening" to God in prayer.
- asking the Lord to increase my faith.
- other:

_____
_____
_____

The Gift of the Written Word
Lesson 13

Sacred Scripture

2 Timothy 3:14-17; 2 Peter 1:19-21; Romans 12:1-2
Catechism: 101-133

Phil had always enjoyed hearing the scriptures read at Mass, but he had rarely opened up the Bible on his own. Then he went on a Catholic Cursillo weekend, and the scriptures suddenly seemed to come alive. Phil went out and bought a paperback Bible, which he began to read every day during his own prayer time. As he became more familiar with scripture passages, he found that they spoke to him in a deeper way than they had ever before.

Phil realized that his daily scripture readings had helped him grow in his faith the day the doctors rushed his wife to the operating room for an emergency cesarean section to deliver their third child. He knew his wife and baby were in danger, but as he prayed, he saw himself in the small boat in the Sea of Galilee with Jesus during the violent storm. He knew that even if Jesus was sleeping, he was in control (Matthew 8:23-27). As he recalled the passage, Phil felt a great peace come over him. He knew the Lord had used that scripture to speak to him personally in a time of crisis.

1. Share about a challenging situation you are experiencing in your own life. What story from the Bible could help you better deal with this problem?

   _____
   _____
   _____
   _____
   _____

2. What is your favorite scripture passage? Why?

   _____
   _____
   _____
   _____
   _____

3. Jesus often used parables to teach us about the truths of the faith. What gospel stories can teach us about God's mercy and forgiveness? What stories can teach us about the Lord's love for sinners?

   _____
   _____
   _____
   _____
   _____

4. In Romans 12:2, St. Paul urges us not to be conformed to this world, but to "be transformed by the renewal of your mind." How can a grounding in biblical truths help us to distinguish godly wisdom from worldly wisdom?

_____

_____

_____

_____

_____

5. Describe an instance when an understanding of the historical and cultural context of a Bible story helped you better grasp the meaning of a passage.

_____

_____

_____

_____

_____

6. Jesus quoted from the scriptures on numerous occasions, including when he was dying on the cross. What does this say about our need to have scripture inscribed on our hearts?

_____

_____

_____

_____

_____

7. How does the living Tradition of the whole Church safeguard our interpretation of scripture? (see Catechism 113)

_____

_____

_____

_____

_____

Action Plan:

This week I will become more a man of the Word by:
- purchasing a Catholic Bible, if I don't already have one, that I can use in my daily prayer time.
- reading and praying over the Mass readings each day.
- joining a Bible study or begin a book-by-book study of the Bible on my own or with a friend.
- other:

_____

_____

Lesson 14

Sacred Tradition

Matthew 28:16-19; Luke 10:1,16; 2 Thessalonians 2:15
Catechism: 74-95

Jack's office was staffed with people from a variety of religious backgrounds, some of whom loved to discuss theology and the differences in doctrine of various Christian denominations. Jack's friend Ralph was an evangelical Christian who often questioned him about Catholic doctrine, especially regarding the Blessed Virgin Mary. Ralph could not understand why Catholics believed that Mary remained a virgin her whole life and was assumed into heaven, body and soul. Ralph said none of these beliefs were in the Bible. When Jack had trouble answering Ralph, he turned to his pastor, who gave him books on the subject.

Ralph learned that unlike many Protestants, who consider scripture as the only source of authority about God, Catholics believe both in the authority of Sacred Scripture and in the authority of Sacred Tradition. Tradition is the Word of God as entrusted to the apostles by Christ, and has been handed down continuously under the inspiration of the Holy Spirit through the bishops in apostolic succession. Jack discovered that even before the New Testament was written down and compiled, the gospel was being proclaimed and bishops were teaching new Christians about the truths of their faith.

1. What does the Church mean when it speaks of Tradition?

_____

_____

_____

_____

_____

2. What is meant by apostolic succession and how is it relevant to Tradition?

_____

_____

_____

_____

_____

_____

3. What is the relationship between Tradition and Sacred Scripture?

_____

_____

_____

_____

_____

4. Why are dogmas established by the Church's Magisterium called "lights along the path of faith"? (see Catechism 89)

_____

_____

_____

_____

_____

_____

5. How do traditional devotions, such as the rosary and the Stations of the Cross, differ from the Tradition handed down from the apostles?

_____

_____

_____

_____

_____

6. How does both Tradition and Sacred Scripture together safeguard the Word of God entrusted to the apostles by Christ?

_____

_____

_____

_____

_____

_____

7. What can we do as Catholics to transmit our faith to the next generation?

_____

_____

_____

_____

_____

Action Plan:

This week I will strive to understand the source of truth by:
- ◉ beginning a systematic study of the Catechism.
- ◉ reading the Vatican II document, *Dogmatic Constitution on Divine Revelation (Dei Verbum)*.
- ◉ reading a respected Catholic author on the subject of Tradition.
- ◉ other:

_____

_____

Lesson 15

The Church's Teaching Authority

Matthew 16:18-20; 28:18-20

Catechism: 85-95; 888-892

Priestly celibacy, women's ordination, the death penalty, abortion—all were "hot" topics that Joe, a recent convert to Catholicism, had never thought much about. As he became more involved in the Church, however, Joe's interest in these issues grew. He decided to research the Church's positions on these and other controversial issues. The process took some time, but Joe was glad he made the effort. As he learned more about the Church's reasoning, he could better understand and appreciate its positions. Even when he struggled in some areas to understand the Church's stance, he realized that the Church's teaching authority was a gift that Catholics should view as a treasure and a source of wisdom in a confused world.

1. Discuss the people and events in your life that helped form your attitude toward authority.

_____

_____

_____

_____

_____

2. What do you think are the attitudes of many Catholics with regard to the teaching authority of the Church?

_____

_____

_____

_____

_____

3. How would you characterize the difference between a sincere search for truth and a search meant only to rationalize or justify a certain belief system?

_____

_____

_____

_____

_____

4. Describe the correlation between the authority given by Jesus to Peter and the other apostles in the Gospel of Matthew, and the authority described in the Catechism (88-95).

_____
_____
_____
_____
_____

5. How would you describe the duties and responsibilities of the Magisterium, or the teaching office, of the Church?

_____
_____
_____
_____
_____

6. How can a better understanding of the role of Magisterium throughout Church history help you grow in appreciation for this authority?

_____
_____
_____
_____
_____

7. How would you describe your own obedience and openness to the authority of the Church?

_____
_____
_____
_____
_____

Action Plan:

This week I will examine my attitude toward the authority of the Church by:
- identifying Church teachings which I don't understand.
- studying Scripture, the Catechism, or other documents of the Church on those particular teachings.
- other:

_____
_____
_____

Serenity Prayer

God grant me
the Serenity to accept the things I cannot change,
the Courage to change the things I can,
and the Wisdom to know the difference;

Living one day at a time;
Accepting hardship as a pathway to peace;
Taking, as Jesus did, this sinful world as it is,
not as I would have it;

Trusting that you will make all things right
if I surrender to your will;
that I may be reasonably happy in this life
and supremely happy with you forever in the next.

The Measure of a Man

Lesson 16

Authentic Christian Men

Psalm 1:1-3; Genesis 1:26-31; John 13:1-14
Catechism: 374-378

A number of years ago there was a best seller entitled *Real Men Don't Eat Quiche*. This book exploited the modern myths of what a real man is all about. Growing up, many of us were taught not to show emotions because "big boys don't cry" or show any kind of weakness. A real man was a rugged individual, a self-made man who pulled himself up by his own bootstraps without needing anything from anybody. The Marlboro Man and John Wayne were our role models, and the real man's theme song was "I Did It My Way."

Did you ever listen to the kinds of questions men ask each other when they first meet? What do you do? Where do you live? Do you know so-and-so? It seems that men tend to define themselves and other men by what they do for a living, what they own, and who they know. The doctor is more respected than a ranch hand, a corporate executive more than a social worker, because of the importance that our society places upon financial success or educational advancement (what we do) rather than who God has created us to be (who we are).

1. According to TV, music, and newspaper ads, what are the characteristics of a real man today? Give an example from an advertisement you've seen.

   _____
   _____
   _____
   _____
   _____

2. What effect does this have on your role as a husband, as a father, and in society?

   _____
   _____
   _____
   _____
   _____

3. Seeing how Jesus treated his disciples, especially his actions in John 13, what might Jesus say are the characteristics of a real man?

   _____
   _____
   _____
   _____
   _____

4. What are some of the influences in society that cause men to lose touch with their own sense that they are created by God in his image?

_____
_____
_____
_____

5. How can relationships with other Christian men help you discover what it means to be an authentic man and follower of Jesus?

_____
_____
_____
_____

6. How would you define happiness? Where do you search for happiness and fulfillment, and where do you find them?

_____
_____
_____
_____

7. If you could be anyone, even a sports celebrity like Michael Jordan or a billionaire like Bill Gates, who would you choose?

_____
_____
_____
_____

Action Plan:

This week I will strive to become a real, authentic Christian man by:
- telling my family that I love them.
- showing generosity to someone in need.
- putting others first at work.
- examining when I was selfish, self-seeking, or greedy.
- other:

_____
_____
_____

Lesson 17

Positive Attitude and Faith

Romans 8:28-39; Hebrews 11:1

Catechism: 222-227

It's interesting that there are men who go through life with, seemingly, everything going for them, yet they always see their glass as half-empty. In contrast, there are other men who face trials and adversities with an attitude of always having a glass that is half-full. What makes the difference?

Gerry Faust, former head football coach at Notre Dame, is one of those guys whose glass is always half-full. One has only to meet Gerry and spend a few minutes with him to come in touch with his zest for life. To him, life is good.

Gerry grew up in a football family, and his lifelong dream was to be head coach at Notre Dame. For many years he thought about it, he dreamed about it, and prayed about it. Then his dream was realized. However, after five seasons with a record of 30-26-1, a record Gerry says was "terrible for Notre Dame," he resigned.

Most men would have been devastated to have their dream end like this, but not Gerry. Even though he was embarrassed and humbled, he says, "I wouldn't trade those years for anything in the world. It was the best five years of my life. And I got through it because of my faith and my family. If you have faith, family, and friends, what more can you ask in life?"

1. How would you describe Gerry Faust, the man, to a friend who had never met him?

_____

_____

_____

_____

_____

2. What are some of the human characteristics that one sees in a person who is an optimist? A pessimist?

_____

_____

_____

_____

_____

3. What factors or events in life help to form a man's disposition and outlook?

_____

_____

_____

_____

_____

The Measure of a Man

4. How do you think a person's sense of faith and his attitude about life are related?

_____

_____

_____

_____

5. What characteristics about Gerry Faust make you think he is a man of faith? What is the evidence in your life that shows you to be a man of faith?

_____

_____

_____

_____

6. What do you think St. Paul meant when he said, "All things work for good for those who love God"? (Romans 8:28). How do you see God working for good in your life?

_____

_____

_____

_____

7. Name three to five ways in which God has been faithful to you throughout your life.

_____

_____

_____

_____

_____

Action Plan:

This week, I will work at eliminating the pessimistic attitudes in my life by:
- ◉ consciously identifying my blessings and thanking God for them often.
- ◉ seeking the source of any bad attitudes or thought patterns I have.
- ◉ selecting the most negative attitude I have and giving it to Jesus every time it arises in my mind or actions.
- ◉ other:

_____

_____

_____

No Choice But to Respond

Lesson 18

A Man of Action

Matthew 25:31-46; Luke 10:30-37; John 15:13

Catechism: 2447

Mike was jogging through the neighborhood as he usually did in the evening, when he noticed a crowd gathering up ahead. He saw smoke billowing out of a house on the corner where an elderly couple, the Johnsons, lived. The crowd was standing around watching, presumably waiting for the fire department to arrive. Mike stopped and asked if the Johnsons were all right. Nobody seemed to know or had even checked. Mike realized that he could not wait for the fire department to arrive since the smoke was increasing rapidly and seemed to be coming out of just about all parts of the house. Running to open the front door, he called out for the Johnsons and thought he heard a faint voice and some coughing from the kitchen area. Mike crawled in under the smoke, found the Johnsons barely conscious in the kitchen, and somehow managed to bring Mrs. Johnson out. Then he went back in and rescued Mr. Johnson.

When the fire department showed up four minutes later, the house was engulfed in flames. One of the firemen told Mike that if he had not done such a brave thing in rescuing the Johnsons, they would have died. Why had he even attempted something so dangerous? Mike thought for a minute and then replied, "They needed help. I had no choice but to respond to someone in need."

1. Were Mike's actions brave or just plain stupid? Why do you think he reacted as he did?

_____

_____

_____

_____

_____

2. Describe a time when you or someone you know came upon a situation that demanded your immediate response. What did you do?

_____

_____

_____

_____

_____

3. In Luke 10, the Samaritan did not hesitate to help his "neighbor." Why do you think the Levite and the priest walked past the man and did not help?

_____

_____

_____

_____

4. What lesson can you draw from the fact that the one who stopped to help was a Samaritan?

_____

_____

_____

_____

_____

5. Jesus clearly reveals in Matthew 25:31-46 that we must put our faith into action. In what practical ways can we do this?

_____

_____

_____

_____

_____

6. What are the pressing needs in your community that need to be addressed? How are you and your parish responding?

_____

_____

_____

_____

_____

7. Has the Holy Spirit ever prompted you to take action in a situation where not to have taken action might have been sinful? How can a committed prayer life lead us to become men of action?

_____

_____

_____

_____

_____

Action Plan:

This week, I will become a man of action by:
- praying for guidance to serve someone in my neighborhood.
- looking for existing needs of others that I have the ability to fulfill.
- deciding on one work of mercy this week and doing it.
- other:

_____

_____

Lesson 19

The Flesh Is Weak

Moral Decision Making

Deuteronomy 30:15-20; Romans 1:18-25
Catechism: 1776-1794; 2045

Ted and Bill had been members of the same small faith group for several years. They had become close friends, sharing some of their most personal concerns with one another. Both of them were married with several children, and as they approached their mid-forties, they began to wrestle with the subject of birth control. In virtually every other aspect of their lives, they had followed the teachings of the Catholic Church, but on this issue they had some reservations.

Ted suggested that they try to resolve the matter by visiting with their pastor. Bill responded with the observation that perhaps their pastor was too conservative, and maybe they should see another priest who would likely be more flexible. Ted agreed. They made several appointments with the other priest, but each time the appointment was canceled through no fault of theirs. They reluctantly concluded that perhaps God was telling them they needed to talk to their own pastor. So they did.

Today, Ted and Bill and their wives are practicing natural family planning, and they feel blessed by the decision they have made.

1. When it comes to difficult moral decisions, there is a tendency for modern Americans to think, "No one's going to tell me what to do. I'll follow my conscience." How would you respond to that statement? (Reading 1776-1794 in the Catechism will be helpful in answering this.)

_____
_____
_____
_____
_____

2. List, in order, the steps that you think should be followed to make a responsible moral decision.

_____
_____
_____
_____
_____

3. Describe the role you think the Bible and Tradition should play in the process of deciding the morality of a particular act.

_____
_____
_____
_____

4. Kids today are wearing bracelets with the letters "WWJD" on them, as a shorthand to the question, "What would Jesus do?" Is this a good standard for you to use in evaluating moral conduct? Explain your answer.

_____

_____

_____

_____

5. What are some safeguards you can use to avoid impulsive immoral behavior?

_____

_____

_____

_____

_____

6. How could prayer be utilized to help make good moral decisions? Share about a time when prayer helped you with a moral dilemma.

_____

_____

_____

_____

_____

7. We think of immoral behavior as things we do wrong, but immorality also includes the failure to take action in certain circumstances. What are some of our society's most blatant "sins of omission"?

_____

_____

_____

_____

_____

Action Plan:

This week, I will do my best to make better moral decisions by:
- reflecting on the Scriptures and the Church's teachings in order to weigh the consequences of any decision before acting.
- seeking spiritual help through prayer or from an informed person in difficult decisions.
- not allowing selfish desires to supersede the moral teachings of the Church.
- always asking, "What would Jesus do in this situation?"
- other:

_____

_____

_____

"Lead Us Not into Temptation"
Lesson 20

Temptation

Genesis 3:1-13; Matthew 26:41; James 1:12-15
Catechism: 2846-2849

George thought of himself as a good, decent God-fearing person. He loved his family, and generally had a good reputation in the community, but George was struggling financially. He worked for a commercial real estate company, and the deals he had tried to put together for the last several months had not worked out. His savings had been depleted, and George began to wonder how he was going to be able to support his family. In fact, he had already talked to an attorney friend about the possibility of filing bankruptcy.

As if in answer to his prayers, a significant transaction came his way. The commission for this deal would make up for the dry spell of the previous months, and then some. He was elated. Then he learned that the property was located on contaminated ground, and if the buyer found out about it, the deal would surely fall through. It was by accident that he had learned of this problem, and the possibility of the buyer finding out was almost nil. This deal would take care of all of his financial problems, and he did have a responsibility to his family. What was he to do?

1. Life is filled with temptations. Describe a major temptation you have faced and how you handled it.

   _____
   _____
   _____
   _____
   _____

2. In Genesis, Adam and Eve try to shift the blame for giving in to temptation. In the above story, how could George do that? How have you done the same thing?

   _____
   _____
   _____
   _____
   _____

3. Most of us have heard the comment that God allows temptation in order to strengthen us. How have struggles with temptation strengthened you?

   _____
   _____
   _____
   _____
   _____

4. Jesus urged his disciples to "watch and pray" (Matthew 26:41). Why is prayer so important when dealing with temptation?

_____
_____
_____
_____
_____

5. Share an instance when prayer has helped you overcome temptation, or when you wished you had prayed.

_____
_____
_____
_____
_____

6. It could be said that yielding to temptation is choosing against God. When does temptation become sin?

_____
_____
_____
_____
_____

7. When tempted in the desert, Jesus began his response each time with, "It is written..." (Matthew 4:4, 4:6, and 4:10). How can you use scripture effectively in dealing with temptation?

_____
_____
_____
_____
_____

Action Plan:

This week, I will do my best not to yield to temptation by:
- being aware of three ways that I fall to temptation and avoid them.
- crying out to God in prayer when I am tempted.
- finding one friend or brother whom I trust and can seek help from when I feel tempted.
- other:

_____
_____
_____

Lesson 21

Habits and the Virtuous Life

Sirach 18:27-33; Philippians 4:8; Titus 2:11-14

Catechism: 1803-1811

Matt was an extrovert and liked to socialize with friends and family. He was funny, interesting, and always the life of the party, especially after a few beers. At one recent party, there was no alcohol. On their way home that night, Matt told his wife Carol, "That was the most boring party I've ever been to." "I'm not surprised," Carol replied. "You just can't seem to relax without a few drinks, can you?" Carol's response took Matt by surprise, and he started to think about what she had said. He realized that his good times depended too much on alcohol. He would have to learn to relax and enjoy people without the crutch of alcohol.

1. What do habits have to do with living a virtuous life?

_____

_____

_____

_____

_____

2. Describe some personal habits that would characterize your style of behavior. How do they relate to the human virtues spoken of in paragraphs 1804-1809 of the Catechism?

_____

_____

_____

_____

_____

3. List habits that are detrimental to living a Christian life. What are their specific dangers?

_____

_____

_____

_____

_____

4. What concrete techniques can you use to break bad habits?

_____

_____

_____

_____

_____

5. How often do you ask for God's grace in seeking to overcome a bad habit? Describe a situation in which you knew that God had helped you to break a bad habit or establish a good one.

_____

_____

_____

_____

_____

6. Discuss specific ways the members of this group can help each other develop these good habits.

_____

_____

_____

_____

_____

7. Identify the good and bad habits we Americans have as a society. How do they impact society?

_____

_____

_____

_____

_____

Action Plan:

This week, I will work on becoming a more virtuous man by:
- asking the Holy Spirit to show me three bad habits and seeking his grace to help me change them.
- selecting the habit I think is most damaging to my living a godly life, and developing a concrete plan to overcome it.
- asking my brothers in this group to pray for me to be able to overcome a specific bad habit.
- seeking the help of a mentor or spiritual director.
- not getting discouraged when I see a bad habit re-surface, but using it as an opportunity to tell God how much I need him and my brothers.
- other:

_____

_____

_____

Lesson 22

Our Actions Speak So Loudly

Integrity

Genesis 39; Proverbs 20:5-7
Catechism: 2464-2470

For years, Troy operated a modest little automotive repair shop in a small town where everyone had grown to trust him with their cars. He was a competent mechanic, and if he said something needed to be repaired on a vehicle, you could count on it. He was also aware of his limitations, particularly with some of the newer foreign cars, and would refer the owner to another shop if he didn't feel he could handle the problem.

As the years passed and Troy got older, he decided to turn the business over to his son, Jesse. One of Jesse's first jobs after Troy retired was to replace a transmission for a young woman. The woman knew absolutely nothing about cars. Jesse, eager to impress his father with his ability to show a good profit, installed a used transmission from a wrecked car, and charged the woman for a new one.

1. What do Jesse's actions say about his integrity?

_____

_____

_____

_____

_____

2. What factors could there be in Jesse's life that would cause him to act differently than Troy?

_____

_____

_____

_____

_____

3. Based on Genesis 39, identify the characteristics that would make you think of Joseph as a man of integrity.

_____

_____

_____

_____

_____

4. In what way did these characteristics play out in Joseph resisting the immoral proposals of Potiphar's wife? Were there any other reasons why he might not have submitted to her?

_____

_____

_____

_____

_____

5. Lies, slander, deception, false witness against another, are all evidence of a lack of integrity in a person. Which of these have you personally encountered in your family or business, and how did you deal with them?

_____

_____

_____

_____

_____

6. Describe the value you think our society places on integrity. How do you think this affects the propensity of the individual in society to be a person of integrity?

_____

_____

_____

_____

_____

_____

7. Under what circumstances, if any, is it ever morally permissible to lie, cheat, or steal, without sacrificing your status as a man of integrity?

_____

_____

_____

_____

_____

Action Plan:

This week, I will address what interferes with my being a man of integrity by:
- examining one way or time that I haven't acted like a man of integrity, repenting of it, and trying to make amends for it.
- choosing two or three ways that I can walk as a man of integrity, especially when no one is looking.
- other:

_____

_____

Lesson 23

Accountability

Genesis 3:1-19; 2 Samuel 12:7-15; Sirach 15:14-15

Catechism: 1730-1736

When his company outgrew its data processing system, Ed recommended a newer, larger system. He hired a couple of new programmers to help make the conversion from one system to the other. However, the lead programmer was not as competent as he had first believed, although he was very good at covering up his inadequacies. Conversion day came, and the system bombed.

Ed's management was livid. Word came from the front office that "somebody's head is going to roll for this." The president of the company met with Ed's immediate superior, John, and asked who was to blame for the fiasco. John pointed out that since Ed was in charge, he was the one who should be fired.

Ed was then called into the president's office and asked the same question: "Who was to blame?" He said, "My employees did the actual work, but as their supervisor, I am ultimately responsible, so if anyone has to be fired, it should be me." However, John was ultimately fired, and Ed was promoted to take his place. Later, the president told Ed that if he had blamed the programmer who had really caused the problem, he would also have been fired for not accepting accountability for his department.

1. Ed and John were both confronted with the same situation, yet responded quite differently. What reasons would you suggest caused the two men to respond as they did?

_____

_____

_____

_____

_____

2. Recall and share instances in your life when you were adversely affected when another person failed to accept accountability for his actions.

_____

_____

_____

_____

_____

3. How do you react when you find yourself "naked" before God—when you get caught?

_____

_____

_____

_____

_____

4. How have you attempted to hide from God and blame others for your sins?

_____
_____
_____
_____
_____

5. What are the consequences on relationships when we shift blame to another for something we have done?

_____
_____
_____
_____
_____
_____

6. What changed David's attitude about accountability to God in the passage from 2 Samuel?

_____
_____
_____
_____
_____
_____

7. What are some specific things you can do to help you become more accountable in your life?

_____
_____
_____
_____
_____
_____

Action Plan:

This week, I will attempt to make amends for when I refused to accept accountability by:
- attempting to repair any damage done.
- seeking forgiveness from a person to whom I shifted blame that was rightfully mine.
- not blaming others, but instead looking for ways to take responsibility for my thoughts, words, and actions.
- other:

_____
_____
_____

Lesson 24

Where Your Treasure Is. . .

The Storing of Treasure

Matthew 6:19-34
Catechism 1911-1912; 2544-2547

Mike and Doris had worked hard for years to be able to afford a lovely home. One morning as they were about to leave for work, their teenage son came screaming into the living room: "I smell smoke! I smell smoke!" Mike and Doris ran upstairs to find that their son's bedroom was thick with smoke. It seems that he had been "sneaking a smoke" before he left for school and had thrown the ignited butt onto the balcony outside his room where it started a fire. Mike hurried to the phone and dialed 911. He and Doris then rushed to the garage and backed their cars out into the street, away from the house.

As they looked back, the second floor was completely engulfed in flames. Their minds raced, thinking about all the belongings that they were losing. Just as the fire trucks arrived, Doris ran into the house and grabbed up her photograph albums. The firemen began to flood the flames with water and after a while, the fire was out. But everything inside had been destroyed by fire, smoke, or water.

1. If this had been your home and you could only save one thing, what would it have been? Why is that object so precious to you?

   _____
   _____
   _____
   _____
   _____

2. Why are we driven to accumulate "things"?

   _____
   _____
   _____
   _____
   _____

3. It's been said that a person's priorities can be determined by looking in his checkbook. What does your checkbook tell about you?

   _____
   _____
   _____
   _____

4. How does your attitude about "wealth" affect your ability to balance your time and energy between your family, your job, and your spiritual life?

_____

_____

_____

_____

5. Why do you think Jesus was so tough on people who had accumulated material possessions?

_____

_____

_____

_____

_____

6. What does the "universal common good" spoken of in the Catechism (1911-1912) have to do with you in real life?

_____

_____

_____

_____

_____

_____

7. How would you describe your eternal life investment portfolio with respect to how you spend free time, how you spend money, and where your thoughts are?

_____

_____

_____

_____

_____

Action Plan:

This week, I will try to discern where I am laying up treasures by:
- ◉ reviewing my checkbook, in detail, to identify my financial priorities.
- ◉ creating a budget that will make better use of my material possessions and income.
- ◉ examining how I support my parish and asking Jesus if I should serve more or give more.
- ◉ other:

_____

_____

Lesson 25

Expressing Emotion
Luke 22:54-62; John 2:13-16; 11:32-36
Catechism: 1771-1775

A man's young son has just been hurt on the soccer field. The father tells him, "Don't show your emotions. Big boys don't cry." A troop leader at a Boy Scout camp out tells one of the boys, "Only sissies are afraid of the dark. Don't let the rest of the boys hear that you are afraid."

How many other examples could be given where boys and young men are taught to suppress their feelings and emotions? Then boys grow into men, and we wonder why they cannot express themselves, especially in intimate relationships like marriage.

1. Discuss with the other participants what you think might be the origins and foundations for the stereotype of the strong, macho, emotionless man.

_____
_____
_____
_____
_____

2. The Catechism (1772) speaks of the principal passions or feelings as love, hatred, desire, fear, joy, sadness, and anger. Which of these feelings are easy or difficult for you to express? Why?

_____
_____
_____
_____
_____

3. Is it easier for you to express your emotions and deepest feelings with another man, or with a woman? Why do you think this is so?

_____
_____
_____
_____

4. After reading Luke 22:54-62, John 2:13-16, and John 11:32-36, how would you describe Jesus (and Peter) in terms of expressing their emotions? Do these expressions show a strength or a weakness?

_____

_____

_____

_____

5. How would you explain paragraph 1773 in the Catechism?

_____

_____

_____

_____

_____

6. How does your ability, or lack of ability, to effectively express your feelings affect the relationship you have with your wife and children? With others?

_____

_____

_____

_____

_____

7. Describe your image of a real man, including how you would see him expressing his emotions. How do you think Jesus expressed his emotions? With his family? With his closest disciples?

_____

_____

_____

_____

Action Plan:

This week I will attempt to better understand the way I express my emotions by:
- being more aware of the feelings I express and how I express them.
- asking my wife to help me with emotions that I might consider not masculine and therefore find difficult to express.
- taking some time to analyze the reasons why I am uncomfortable with a particular emotion or feeling.
- other:

_____

_____

_____

Lesson 26 — Showing the Sword

A Man's Anger

Matthew 5:21-22,38-48, 21:12-13; Ephesians 4:26-27

Catechism: 1931; 2608

We live in a culture that places a great premium on "keeping cool." We congratulate people for keeping their composure at funerals. A presidential candidate once faded from contention after he cried over verbal attacks made on his wife. Any statement made with emotion is frequently discounted.

Showing anger is almost the greatest taboo. "Don't get so upset" is a common reaction when someone displays anger. However, the truth is that anger is a natural, God-given emotion. Even the Lord is sometimes portrayed in scripture as being angry (see Exodus 4:14; Numbers 12:9; Deuteronomy 9:20). Jesus became angry as well (see Matthew 21:12-13).

Stifling appropriate anger can cause more harm than expressing it. The issue is not that all anger is bad, but that we learn how to control and communicate it properly, positively, and constructively. One of the keys is understanding the source of our anger in each situation.

1. How can Jesus' teaching about anger in Matthew 5:22 be reconciled with his action in cleansing the Temple in Matthew 21:12-13?

2. What are the main causes of a man's anger? What makes you angry?

3. When is anger appropriate? Describe a time in your life when you feel you were appropriately angry. What were the results of your anger, both positive and negative?

4. When is anger sin? Share a time in your life when you were inappropriately angry. What were the consequences for you and the one against whom your anger was directed?

_____

_____

_____

_____

_____

5. What can you do to control inappropriate anger?

_____

_____

_____

_____

_____

6. What are some effective ways of responding when another directs his or her anger at you?

_____

_____

_____

_____

_____

7. Occasionally, one meets a person who radiates a sense of serenity and peace. How do you think this person deals with anger, and how can you become such a person?

_____

_____

_____

_____

_____

Action Plan:

This week, I will work on controlling inappropriate anger by:
- ⦿ praying for God's help in moments of distress when I usually get angry.
- ⦿ trying to recognize two situations that normally make me angry, and placing them at Jesus' feet.
- ⦿ developing a plan to act differently in these situations, such as walking away or taking some time before I try to speak.
- ⦿ other:

_____

_____

Lesson 27

Forgiveness

Matthew 5:23-24, 18:15-17,21-35
Catechism: 982; 2842-2844

Tom had spent three days at a spiritual retreat. While forgiveness had almost never been mentioned during the retreat, every time he prayed his thoughts would turn to Don, his former business partner. They had split up six years earlier, and even though they were neighbors, they hardly ever spoke to one another. During the retreat, Tom had a sense that God was telling him to reconcile with Don.

When the retreat ended and Tom returned to work, he called Don and invited him to lunch. During their meal together, they exchanged small talk. Tom was more than a little nervous. When Don got up to leave, Tom stopped him, saying, "Don, there's something else we need to talk about." Tom described the anger he had long harbored toward Don and expressed his regret. Don accepted Tom's apology and asked for Tom's forgiveness. Don's parting words were, "You know, Tom, I have always loved you like a brother, even after we split up."

1. Why is forgiving another person so difficult? What are the things that get in the way?

_____
_____
_____
_____
_____

2. So many times we harbor resentment against people who have rejected us. What are some practical, helpful ways of dealing with rejection?

_____
_____
_____
_____
_____

3. There are some people who feel that their life is so evil that God cannot possibly forgive them. How would you counsel them in light of paragraph 982 of the Catechism?

_____
_____
_____
_____
_____

4. From the beginning of time, revenge has been a fundamental motivation for fallen man. Discuss a situation in your life in which revenge affected you.

_____
_____
_____
_____
_____

5. What are the implications of praying the Our Father and receiving Communion when there is a relationship in your life that is not reconciled? What should you do?

_____
_____
_____
_____
_____

6. The Parable of the Unforgiving Servant (Matthew 18:21-35) is played out everyday in our society. Are you personally aware of an event that fits this parable? What were the results?

_____
_____
_____
_____
_____

7. What has been your experience with the Sacrament of Reconciliation? What role has it played, or could it play, in helping you to become a more forgiving person?

_____
_____
_____
_____
_____

Action Plan:

This week I will strive to be a more forgiving person by:
- ⦿ asking my brothers to pray that I might be more forgiving.
- ⦿ praying daily for someone against whom I harbor resentment or enmity.
- ⦿ seeking reconciliation with any "enemy" I might have before receiving Communion.
- ⦿ other:

_____
_____
_____

Lesson 28

Vigilance

Luke 12:35-48; 1 Thessalonians 4:13-18; 5:1-11; Revelation 21:1-7
Catechism: 673

There were three devils in training who were about to go to earth for some on-the-job experience as devil interns. Before they left, their supervisor asked them what techniques they planned to use to get people to sin.

The first devil said, "I think I'll take the classical approach. I'll tell people there is no God, so sin up a storm and enjoy life." The second devil said, "Well I think I'll use a more subtle approach. I'll tell people there is no hell, so sin up a storm and enjoy life." The third devil, the smartest of his whole class, said, "I think I'll just get the people to relax by telling them there's no hurry, so sin up a storm and enjoy life."

1. Jesus said, "Blessed are those servants whom the master finds vigilant on his arrival" (Luke 12:37). What do you think it means to be "vigilant"?

_____

_____

_____

_____

_____

2. What are you doing to be found vigilant upon the Master's return?

_____

_____

_____

_____

_____

3. List four areas in your life where God wants you to be vigilant, and about which God has made you a steward, and over which you will be held accountable.

_____

_____

_____

_____

_____

4. Reflect on the Second Coming as part of God's plan for creation (Catechism 673). In what ways can the thought of Jesus' return infuse us with hope?

_____
_____
_____
_____
_____

5. How does our understanding of the end times differ from that of the early Christians? (see 1 Thessalonians 4:15)

_____
_____
_____
_____
_____

6. Think about what motivates you to be prepared for the Lord's return. Is it out of love for God, fear of his punishment, or anything else?

_____
_____
_____
_____
_____

7. If you received a phone call from a reliable source, stating that Jesus was returning to earth next Saturday at noon, how would your plans for the rest of this week change? How would you spend your time over the next few days?

_____
_____
_____
_____
_____

Action Plan:

This week, I will try to become more vigilant by:
- acting this week in my prayer, family, and workplace as if Jesus will come tonight.
- trying to imagine what it must be like in heaven.
- taking stock of the things that separate me from God and meditating on the love that the Lord has for me.
- other:

_____
_____
_____

Lesson 29

Risks and Consequences

Matthew 14:25-33; Acts 4:1-22

Catechism: 2471-2473

Father Damien De Veuster was a nineteenth-century Belgian priest who spent many years ministering to a leper colony on the island of Molokai in Hawaii. When he arrived there in 1873, the colony was a living hell, filled with hopelessness and despair. Father Damien sought to bring dignity and joy to the community, helping them to build villages and to farm. At the outset, he decided he would fully interact with the lepers and took no precautions against contracting the disease. Eventually he came down with leprosy himself, and died in 1889 at the age of forty-nine. In serving the most needy, Father Damien willingly risked—and lost—his own life.

1. What motivated Father Damien to risk his own life in ministering to the lepers?

_____

_____

_____

_____

_____

_____

2. What kinds of risks are intrinsically linked to committing our own lives to loving and serving others?

_____

_____

_____

_____

_____

3. Try to place yourself inside Peter's head in Matthew 14:25-33 and imagine his feelings when Jesus invited him to come on the water. Describe these feelings. Repeat this process with the reading from Acts 4.

_____

_____

_____

_____

_____

_____

4. When witnessing to your faith, are you more likely to respond with the attitude of Peter in Matthew, or in Acts?

_____

_____

_____

_____

_____

5. What's the one thing God could ask of you that would make you feel very uncomfortable? Could this be God's way of inviting you to get out of the boat?

_____

_____

_____

_____

_____

6. Share a personal example of someone you know who took a risk based on his faith in God.

_____

_____

_____

_____

_____

7. Do you think the Catholic Church is a place for adventuresome men who are willing to take risks? What if there were financial rewards involved? Explain.

_____

_____

_____

_____

_____

Action Plan:

I will take a risk and stretch myself spiritually in the next week by:
- sharing my faith story with someone with whom I have never discussed my faith.
- discussing a troublesome faith issue or a doubt about my faith with my spouse or, if I am not married, with a best friend.
- acting on those issues in my life that will put me at risk for following Jesus and his teachings.
- other:

_____

_____

Lesson 30
Strength through Weakness

Letting Go

Philippians 2:3-11; 2 Corinthians 12:7-10
Catechism: 519-521

Robert was used to having what he wanted. He had worked hard to earn his position in the community and at work, and was looked up to by others. Robert had "made it." He was able to have the best and to provide the best for himself and his family. When Robert's daughter, Bristol, was born, his life changed. Robert and his wife realized something was terribly wrong with Bristol, and after much searching and testing, even the best doctors and hospitals could do nothing. For ten years, Robert loved and cared for Bristol and prayed unceasingly for her. He cared for her every need as she slowly withered away until finally she went to be with the Lord. Nothing Robert did stopped the slow, debilitating death of his daughter. All the power, money, and prestige in the world could not change that. Yet, in his "weakness," Robert was able to provide what Bristol needed most-a loving, caring father who was always there for her and who would not abandon her in her need.

1. Recall a time when you relied on your own wits, power, or position to control things or events around you. Now recall a time when things were "out of your control." How were you able to make it through the time when you were not in control of events or people?

_____

_____

_____

_____

_____

2. Discuss the fears you face in being "out of control." How can your relationship with Jesus help you to confront these fears?

_____

_____

_____

_____

_____

3. The humility and obedience of Jesus led him to become a servant, to take on human form, and to death on a cross. What does this mean to you?

_____

_____

_____

_____

_____

4. How do you reconcile the model that Jesus offers with the expectations of your family? Society?

_____

_____

_____

_____

_____

5. Paul was wise, and was a powerful speaker and writer. However, he saw his own pride as an obstacle. What obstacles do you face that may prevent God from fully using you?

_____

_____

_____

_____

_____

6. What "thorn in the flesh" do you think God has given to you? Do you see this thorn as a burden or as a blessing? Why?

_____

_____

_____

_____

_____

7. "My grace is sufficient for you, for power is made perfect in weakness" (2 Corinthians 12:9). What does this mean to you? How difficult is it to give up control and "let go and let God"?

_____

_____

_____

_____

_____

Action Plan:

This week I will examine those areas in my life where I desire power, prestige, or control by:
- making a list of those elements in my life that I think I control.
- talking with my spouse or a close friend about my propensity to control.
- asking God to send the Holy Spirit to help me overcome the desire to be in control.
- other:

_____

_____

_____

Man and Family

Lesson 31

Mapping Out a Vision

Family Vision

Proverbs 11:14; Acts 16:25-34

Catechism: 1655-1657

Mike is the owner of a very successful business that has a reputation as a highly ethical company providing an excellent product at a reasonable price. The company is known for taking care of its customers, and as a result, is highly profitable. Mike attributes his success to having a very clear vision, early on, about the kind of business he wanted to run, developing a plan to make it happen, and paying constant attention to how well the plan was working in the reality of everyday life.

By contrast, Mike's family was a mess. It wasn't a bad family, but there never seemed to be the kind of unity or affection he thought a strong family should have. One evening, as he was sitting in his study after an unpleasant exchange with his two sons, Mike wondered how he could be so successful in his business and, at the same time, struggle so much with his family.

1. What would you suggest to Mike as being a problem with his family?

_____

_____

_____

_____

_____

2. How would you describe the direction of your family at this point?

_____

_____

_____

_____

_____

3. Discuss Mike's approach to developing a successful business, and what tools he employs there that could be helpful in dealing with his family.

_____

_____

_____

_____

_____

4. In Acts, there are numerous references to a person being converted, then desiring that his "whole household should be saved." How do you show your desire for your family's salvation?

_____
_____
_____
_____
_____

5. Many individuals have a personal vision statement. What would you include in a family vision statement?

_____
_____
_____
_____
_____
_____

6. How would this vision statement compare to the reality of your family life today?

_____
_____
_____
_____
_____

7. Discuss the importance of a man and his wife having a well-defined plan for their family?

_____
_____
_____
_____
_____

Action Plan:

This week, I will demonstrate more concern for the future of my family by:
- beginning to pray for each member of my family.
- praying daily that my children will respond to the call that God gives to them in their life.
- discussing with my wife the possibility of developing a plan for our family's salvation.
- other:

_____
_____
_____

Setting Family Goals

Listed below are some goals you might want to consider for your family that can help you grow together in love and unity. Discuss which goals your family should focus on. After some discussion, your family may come up with other goals that are more appropriate. From time to time, evaluate your progress to see how much God has done for you.

1. We will be open and teachable in our family and allow the teachings of Jesus to guide and form us.

2. We will attend church together as a family on Sunday and try to pray together for a few minutes each day.

3. We will grow in love and appreciation for one another.

4. We will talk with and value one another during our meals together.

5. We will be honest with one another, never allowing lies or deceit to have a place in our family.

6. We will work together for the common good of the family and not just for our own personal interest.

7. We will do our fair share of the work in our house without complaining.

8. We will forgive one another and not let past hurts rule our family.

9. We will not allow critical attitudes, cynicism, or negative humor to threaten our relationships with one another.

10. We will not let anger and moods darken the atmosphere of our home.

Lesson 32

Choose This Day Whom You Will Serve

Leading the Family

Deuteronomy 6:1-9; Joshua 24:14-15; Ephesians 5:21-6:4
Catechism: 2202-2206; 2223

It was 9:00 p.m. on Friday evening when the phone rang at the home of Larry and Beverly. It was the most frightening phone call they had ever received. "Hello. This is Sergeant Blocker at the Police Department. Could you please come down to the station? We have arrested your sixteen-year-old son, Rodney, for attempting to hold up a convenience store and for possession of drugs."

A thousand things raced through Larry's mind at one time. "How could this have happened? I've worked my fingers to the bone to provide the very best for my son. He's never lacked anything: best schools, best clothes, membership to the country club, high-class summer camps. What more could I have done for him?"

1. Where might Larry have gone wrong in influencing Rodney's behavior?

_____

_____

_____

_____

_____

2. What kind of difficulties does a man face in trying to serve as the spiritual leader of his family? What things can get in his way?

_____

_____

_____

_____

_____

3. The author of Joshua implores us to "decide today whom you will serve" (24:15). What false gods do we sometimes serve, and lead our family to serve?

_____

_____

_____

_____

_____

4. How are we as husbands to love our wives? Does this model of leadership or authority fit with the modern view of what a real man is?

_____

_____

_____

_____

_____

5. Reflecting on the readings, especially paragraph 2223 in the Catechism, in what specific ways are we, as fathers, to lead our children?

_____

_____

_____

_____

_____

6. Where does a man's authority as a family leader actually come from? How should a man go about finding the direction he can give his family?

_____

_____

_____

_____

_____

7. In what ways might a father's leadership differ or contrast with a wife's leadership in the home? In what ways are they similar?

_____

_____

_____

_____

_____

Action Plan:

This week, I will attempt to be a better servant leader in my family by:
- paying more attention to my wife and children and their needs.
- spending time reflecting on the kind of servant leader I have been to my family.
- identifying one area where I need improvement, and working on improving in that area.
- other:

_____

_____

_____

Lesson 33

The Man as a Warrior

Ephesians 6:10-20; 1 Peter 5:8-11
Catechism: 407-409; 2228

In his book, *Point Man*, author Steve Farrar says: "If you are a husband/father, then you are in a war. War has been declared upon the family, on your family and mine. Leading a family through the chaos of American culture is like leading a small patrol through enemy-occupied territory."

Mr. Farrar also cites the following quote from Dr. James Dobson, who said in 1980: "It is my opinion that our very survival as a people will depend upon the presence or absence of masculine leadership in millions of homes. . . . I believe, with everything within me, that husbands hold the keys to the preservation of the family."

Farrar adds that, "When [the enemy] wants to destroy a family, he focuses on the man. For if he can neutralize the man. . .he has neutralized the family. . . . What that means is that we should expect to be attacked. We should expect extreme temptation to come our way. When you get serious about leading your family, you will be opposed."

1. Farrar speaks of husbands and fathers being in a war. How does this "war" impact your daily life?

_____
_____
_____
_____
_____

2. What evil is attacking your family—its unity, love of God and one another?

_____
_____
_____
_____
_____

3. What weapons does a husband/father have available for the battle to save his family?

_____
_____
_____
_____
_____

4. How do you and your wife work together to protect your children from evil? Describe the specific steps you have taken to combat evil in your family.

_____

_____

_____

_____

_____

5. How can we as a group of brothers help our families in the fight against evil?

_____

_____

_____

_____

_____

6. The Catechism (2228) speaks of the responsibility of providing for the spiritual as well as the physical needs of your children. In what practical ways can you do this?

_____

_____

_____

_____

_____

7. It's been said that sometimes the most effective evil is not that which is clearly bad, but the good that isn't good enough. What "good" in your family keeps your family members from the ultimate good which is God?

_____

_____

_____

_____

_____

Action Plan:

Over the next week, I will be more alert to potential spiritual dangers to my family by:
- paying closer attention to the programs that our family watches on TV.
- staying more aware of who my children's friends are and what they do together.
- informing myself about what the children are being taught in school.
- paying more attention to the influence I have on my family through my own life.
- other:

_____

_____

_____

Lesson 34

Bone of My Bones

A Man and His Wife

Genesis 2:18-25; Ephesians 5:21-33
Catechism: 2334-2335; 2363-2364

Steve and Beth met for dinner with Larry and Susan, neighbors who were in their parish RCIA program. The conversation was lively and interesting. Larry told of the months that he and Susan spent studying scripture and the Catechism together. They would meet at a park every day during their lunch hour, and share about their prayer or go over their group discussion questions. On Saturday mornings, they made sure to block out time to pray together and read scripture. Susan told Steve and Beth of the excitement of sharing this journey with Larry, of conversations on religion with her co-workers, of hours of prayer with Larry as they asked God to reveal the direction for their lives.

When the evening came to a close, Steve and Beth got into their car and began driving away. After several minutes of silence, Beth turned to Steve and said the exact words he had been thinking: "I've never met a married couple that was so unified."

1. Describe the most significant areas of unity or "oneness" which you have with your wife.

_____

_____

_____

_____

_____

2. The expression, "living together separately," is sometimes used to describe a lack of unity in a marriage. How would you explain this expression, perhaps even with an example from a time or period in your own marriage?

_____

_____

_____

_____

_____

3. Describe the extent to which you do or do not put the interests of your wife ahead of your own interests. Why?

_____

_____

_____

_____

_____

4. What can you do to help your wife to grow in holiness and love of the Lord?

_____

_____

_____

_____

_____

5. Describe how you and your wife go about discerning what is God's will for your relationship and for your household.

_____

_____

_____

_____

_____

6. In your own words, give your understanding of how a Christian husband exercises his authority under the guidelines set forth in Ephesians 5.

_____

_____

_____

_____

_____

7. Describe some specific ways a man and his wife can help one another live up to their responsibilities as Christian spouses.

_____

_____

_____

_____

_____

Action Plan:

This week I will try to build up and strengthen my marriage by:
- ◉ telling my wife that I love her each day and giving her a kiss.
- ◉ inviting my wife to pray with me each day for our marriage and family.
- ◉ finding ways to continue to court my wife as I did before we were married.
- ◉ praying daily for my wife.
- ◉ other:

_____

_____

_____

Lesson 35

The Sexuality of a Man

1 Corinthians 7:3-5; Ephesians 5:25-31
Catechism: 372; 2361-2363; 2366-2370

If marriage can be defined as the mutual self-giving between a man and a woman before God, the fullest expression of this self-giving is sexual intercourse. In the sexual act, the man and woman literally become one flesh. In doing so, they also encounter the creative power of God. Out of their union they can transmit new life, a child who reflects the characteristics of the father and mother. As man and woman are made in God's image, so a child is made in the image of the father and mother.

It's incredible that God's plan of salvation involves the sharing of the power to create human life with men and women. The Catholic Church calls us to be good stewards of this power. The Church also acts as a safeguard to ensure that the beauty and power of God's plan of creation are not compromised by sin.

1. In the reading from Ephesians 5, there is a clear indication that a husband is largely responsible for the sexual purity of his wife. What are some ways a husband can fulfill this responsibility?

_____

_____

_____

_____

_____

2. How can a man help make sure that in the act of sexual intercourse with his wife, he is giving himself and not just taking?

_____

_____

_____

_____

_____

3. Wives desire to have affection from their husbands which is not always connected with sex. What are some ways that you can show her affection on a regular basis?

_____

_____

_____

_____

_____

4. To what extent have you, or could you, be affected by pornography, sexual fantasies, or other areas of sexual temptation?

_____

_____

_____

_____

_____

5. How can men discern God's will with respect to having more children?

_____

_____

_____

_____

_____

6. Are there attitudes that you may have picked up growing up that negatively affect your sexual relationship with your wife? If so, discuss how you can overcome them.

_____

_____

_____

_____

_____

7. If you were asked to give a talk on chastity to a group of teenagers, what points would you make in favor of saving sexual intercourse for marriage?

_____

_____

_____

_____

_____

Action Plan:

Over the next week I will attempt to better understand and express my sexuality by:
- studying what the scriptures say about sexuality.
- studying the documents of the Church that have to do with sexuality.
- having a candid conversation with my wife about our sexual relationship.
- other:

_____

_____

_____

Lesson 36

Fidelity

Genesis 39:1-23; 2 Samuel 11:1-27; Matthew 5:27-30
Catechism: 2364-2365; 2380-2381

In the movie *Fatal Attraction*, Michael Douglas plays a character named Dan. Dan is portrayed as an obviously loving husband and doting father who has to stay in the city because of a business meeting, while his wife and daughter go to the country for the weekend. Attending the business meeting is an attractive young woman named Alex, played by Glenn Close. Dan briefly met Alex the night before at a client cocktail party.

After the meeting, Dan gets caught in a torrential rain storm as he leaves the building, and his umbrella doesn't work. Alex spots him and offers to share her umbrella. They duck into a restaurant for a drink to wait out the rain, wind up having dinner together, and end up at Alex's apartment. This is the beginning of a weekend of an unbridled adulterous affair.

Complications begin when Dan wants to call it quits after the weekend and Alex wants the relationship to continue. The rest of the story is about how this one indiscreet weekend almost destroyed Dan's wife, their child, and their marriage.

1. What do you think could make a man who appears to be a faithful and loving husband risk his marriage for a weekend with a stranger?

   _____
   _____
   _____
   _____
   _____

2. What are the dangerous situations that men face every day that could tempt them into an experience like the one described in the opening story?

   _____
   _____
   _____
   _____
   _____

3. In the readings from Genesis and 2 Samuel, Joseph and David are both faced with the temptation to violate a marriage. Discuss the character of these two men and why you think each of them reacted as they did.

   _____
   _____
   _____
   _____
   _____

4. Describe a situation involving temptation that you were aware of and how it was handled. How can a man protect himself against falling to a temptation that would violate his marriage?

_____
_____
_____
_____
_____

5. What does it mean for a man to practice fidelity? What ways other than sexually can a man be unfaithful to his wife?

_____
_____
_____
_____
_____

6. What are the implications for you personally of the comments made by Jesus (Matthew 5:27-28) regarding adultery committed in a man's heart?

_____
_____
_____
_____
_____

7. What, in your opinion, is the greatest factor leading to so much infidelity today, even among practicing Christians?

_____
_____
_____
_____

Action Plan:

This week I will be more alert to the dangers of infidelity by:
- making a mental inventory of tempting situations to avoid.
- considering the consequences of committing adultery, especially the effect on my wife.
- calling to mind the non-sexual ways in which I am unfaithful.
- praying daily to be strong in avoiding temptations.
- spending time each day considering how much I love my family and how important they are to me.
- other:

_____
_____
_____

Lesson 37

In My Father's House

A Man and His Father

Deuteronomy 5:16; Sirach 3:1-16; Luke 2:21-52
Catechism: 2200; 2214

Jim was struggling with his past while trying to be a good father and husband in the present. His dad was a devoted husband, but had a problem with alcohol and was largely absent while Jim was growing up. Now, Jim was dealing with the responsibilities of being a father of three without a role model or set of instructions to help. He loved and cared for his children, and provided for their physical and spiritual needs, but struggled with nurturing and supporting them emotionally. He even felt fear and inadequacy at those times when he was needed most to "just love and hold his kids," rather than to instruct, teach, or admonish them.

Jim began to realize that his view of God had been shaped by his experiences with his own father. He saw God as a loving but distant Father who was unapproachable and not actively involved in his life. Jim struggled with trying to be the perfect father and doing it all on his own (and failing miserably) until finally, when things got so desperate for him, he begged God to come into his life and change his heart. God immediately started working in Jim's life, first by showing what a loving, caring, and always present Father he is. Step by step and day by day, God has helped Jim in his own vocation as a father by showing him his everlasting and unconditional love. Jim now strives to show this kind of love to his children.

1. List five adjectives that describe your father. What is your most vivid memory of him?

_____

_____

_____

_____

_____

2. What was the most meaningful spiritual experience you had with your father?

_____

_____

_____

_____

_____

3. In Christianity, Jesus is our model. Considering Jesus as a human son, what do you see as the ideal relationship between a father and a son?

_____

_____

_____

_____

_____

4. In what ways did you honor your father as a child and teenager? As an adult?

_____

_____

_____

_____

5. Describe the legacies of fatherhood and faith that your father has passed on to you. Was this legacy positive, or one on which you need to improve?

_____

_____

_____

_____

_____

6. How has your relationship with your father affected your understanding of God the Father? Are you absolutely sure that God the Father genuinely loves you and wants to help you each day?

_____

_____

_____

_____

7. Identify any issues that have not been resolved between you and your father.

_____

_____

_____

_____

Action Plan:

This week I will attempt to reconcile any unresolved problems with my earthly father, whether living or dead, by:

- paying him a personal visit, calling him on the phone, or writing him a note or letter.
- asking for forgiveness in prayer.
- saying "I love you" to him.
- thanking him for a specific contribution he made to my life.
- other:

_____

_____

Lesson 38

Persevering in Love

Teaching Our Children

Deuteronomy 6:4-9; Proverbs 22:6; Ephesians 6:1-4

Catechism: 2221-2228

St. Monica was the mother of St. Augustine, a brilliant man, a bishop, and a doctor of the Church who lived in the fourth century. However, Augustine was not always a "saint." He lived many years with a concubine and fathered a son out of wedlock. He consulted astrologers and belonged to a heretical religion. Meanwhile, St. Monica, a devout Christian, prayed daily for her son and would not abandon him. Even after St. Augustine tricked his mother and sailed from Carthage to Rome without her, she followed him and would not give up on him. St. Monica's steadfast devotion and love, and her unceasing prayers, sacrifice, and tears, eventually bore fruit: both St. Augustine—then 32 years old—and his son, Adeodatus, were baptized and came to the Church at Easter in the year 387. St. Monica is an ideal model of an unselfish parent, and the fruits of her labor have had a lasting effect on the Church today.

1. Why do you think St. Monica did not give up on her son? How do you suppose she was able to persevere for so long even when it seemed hopeless?

_____

_____

_____

_____

_____

2. What are your most important duties of a parent in the raising of your children?

_____

_____

_____

_____

_____

3. How have you experienced the wisdom of Proverbs 22:6, either in your life or in the life of someone you know? Is the easiest way always the best way? Explain.

_____

_____

_____

_____

_____

4. Why is it important to teach children the commands God gives us? What are some of the methods we can use to teach? (see Deuteronomy 6:7-9)

_____

_____

_____

_____

_____

5. How can fathers fulfill the instructions of St. Paul in Ephesians 6:1-4 to bring children up with the training and instruction of the Lord, yet without provoking their anger?

_____

_____

_____

_____

_____

6. The Catechism talks about parents evangelizing their children (2225). What can parents do to share and teach the Good News to their children?

_____

_____

_____

_____

_____

7. The Catechism also instructs parents and children alike to be generous and tireless in forgiving. How can parents best teach forgiveness? Give an example.

_____

_____

_____

_____

_____

Action Plan:

I will accept the responsibility that God has given me as a parent and provide not only for the physical needs of my children, but for their spiritual needs by:
- examining the role model I provide for my family and addressing any areas of bad influence.
- taking inventory of my role as a parent in light of the Catechism and Scripture references in this lesson plan.
- praying with my wife about being more godly parents.
- other:

_____

_____

_____

Lesson 39

The Family As Domestic Church

Colossians 3:12-21; Ephesians 4:25-32

Catechism: 2204-2206

In many parishes on the Feast of the Holy Family, married deacons are invited to preach at the Masses. When his pastor asked him to give the homily that day, Deacon John wondered what he could talk about. He knew that many families—his own included—find it a challenge to live up to the standard of the Holy Family. One day as he paged through the parish directory trying to find a phone number, he glanced down at the name of a family he had known for many years, who had shepherded four children to adulthood. They had experienced their share of trials and sorrows, but always they had clung to the Lord for their strength.

As John flipped through the directory, other family names caught his eye. These were families who prayed together, shared Scripture with their children, or gave each other blessings as they left for school or work. He knew these parents involved their children in charitable works, and were willing to swim against the tide of society to teach Christian morals and ethics to their children. He realized he had plenty of material for his sermon. These families were Christian witnesses to the power of God in their lives. They lived as holy families, just as the Holy Family had, in the presence of Jesus.

1. In what ways do the families described in the above story function as a domestic church?

_____

_____

_____

_____

_____

2. According to Colossians 3:12-21, what are the characteristics that distinguish the Christian from the rest of society? What happens when families live out these characteristics?

_____

_____

_____

_____

3. How does your family incorporate the characteristics found in Colossians into its daily life?

_____

_____

_____

_____

_____

4. Which of these characteristics are most difficult to practice in your family? Why?

_____

_____

_____

_____

_____

5. On what occasions does your family pray and/or read scripture together? What are some ways to make this happen on a more regular basis?

_____

_____

_____

_____

_____

6. The Catechism (2205) states that the Christian family has both an evangelizing and missionary task. How can your family fulfill this duty within the parish community? Within the community at large?

_____

_____

_____

_____

_____

7. How does viewing God as our Father contribute to our understanding of the family as the domestic church?

_____

_____

_____

_____

_____

Action Plan:

This week I will try to assist my family in better understanding the nature of a godly family by:
- establishing a formal time for prayer together at least once per week.
- discussing with them what it means for us to be a domestic church.
- helping them to understand the connection between worshipping at Mass together and home life.
- other:

_____

_____

Lesson 40

Spending Time Together

Deuteronomy 6:4-9; Malachi 3:23-24; Ephesians 6:1-4
Catechism: 2207

Brian volunteered to help his parish promote a workshop on marriage and family life. He was quickly informed that the parish needed him to copy, sort and mail 900 brochures. This had to be done right away. Knowing that he couldn't complete this task on time by himself, Brian recruited his three children to assist him. They gathered in the parish conference room around a big table and started an assembly line.

For almost four hours, they worked together, joking with one another, laughing, telling stories, discussing what was going on in each of their lives. It was great just being together. "Before the industrial age," Brian thought to himself, "this must have been what family life was like all the time. Parents and children worked alongside one another, instead of the father disappearing for long periods of time into some place called the factory, or the shop, or the office.

"I've got to spend more time with my children," Brian said to himself. He wasn't thinking about sitting in bleachers or chairs watching his children while they performed, but really being with them. This would take commitment and serious changes in his life, but he knew it would be worth it.

1. Describe one of the fondest childhood memories you have of family time together. How has that activity impacted your life as an adult?

_____

_____

_____

_____

_____

2. How often is your family able to eat dinner together? In what ways does sitting down at meal times contribute to the family's sense of togetherness and unity?

_____

_____

_____

_____

_____

3. What are some of the specific activities you and your children have successfully engaged in together. Describe the benefits to the family.

_____

_____

_____

_____

4. Identify some of the obstacles that prevent you from spending more time with your family.

_____

_____

_____

_____

_____

5. One of the Ten Commandments is to keep holy the Lord's Day. Describe your successes and failures in making Sunday a special day to focus on God and family.

_____

_____

_____

_____

_____

_____

6. It's said that the quality of time spent with children is more important than the quantity of that time. Indicate whether you agree or disagree with this statement and explain your reason.

_____

_____

_____

_____

_____

_____

7. If your doctor told you that you only had ninety days to live, what would you do differently with respect to your family?

_____

_____

_____

_____

_____

Action Plan:

This week I will pay more attention to the time I spend with my family by:
- analyzing the time I spend at work and other non-family activities.
- actually involving myself with them instead of just "being there."
- taking a walk with my wife and learning more about her interests.
- talking to each of my children one-on-one.
- other:

_____

_____

_____

Signposts

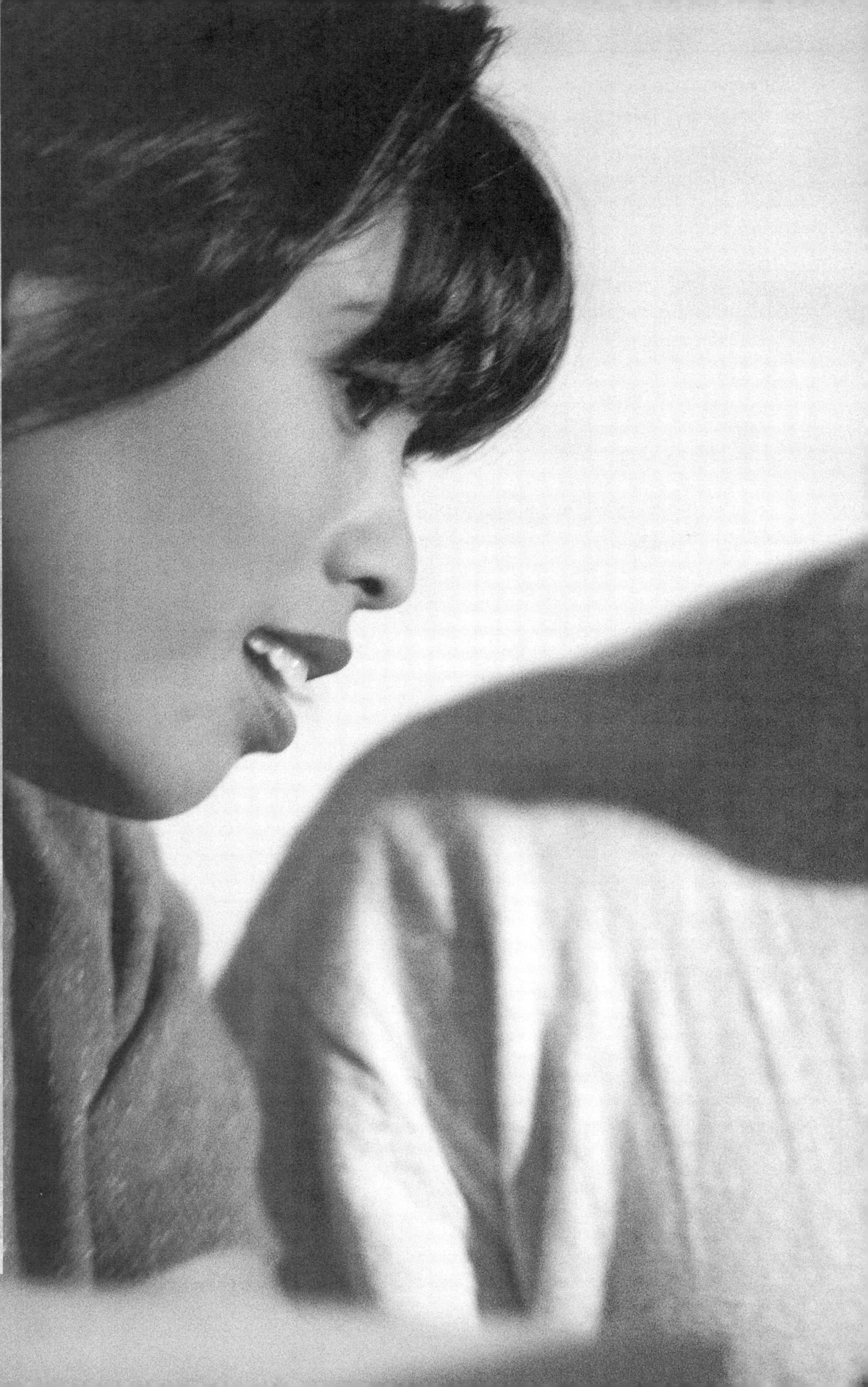

Man and His World

Lesson 41
A Question of Balance

A Man and His Job

Genesis 3:14-19; Matthew 25:14-30; 2 Thessalonians 3:10
Catechism: 2427-2428; 2460

Mike was smart, young, ambitious, and anxious to climb the corporate ladder. He worked in a highly competitive industry, and the key to success was forming relationships with the potential buyers of the services that his firm offered.

Mike's hard work paid off when he was made general manager of one of the company's offices. Unfortunately, the cost for the promotion was significant. The long hours and dedication to his job left little time for him to pay attention to his family, and after eleven years and two children, his wife divorced him.

Mike is now remarried, his wife is pregnant and the pattern is repeating itself. The long hours are problematic, but the straw that broke the camel's back was his coming home more than once at two or three o'clock in the morning. He had been with clients in a strip bar, trying to develop business relationships and loyalty with potential customers. When his wife found out where Mike had been, she asked, "What kind of business could possibly be transacted while drinking all night in a strip bar?" "Calm down, honey," he replied. "It's what everybody in business does."

1. In the Catechism (2427), we are taught that, through work, we participate in God's creative activities as well as honor the gifts and talents we have been given by God. How does Mike's attitude toward his work contrast with God's view?

_____

_____

_____

_____

_____

2. The Parable of the Talents (Matthew 25:14-30) speaks of our duties with regard to the gifts and talents we have been given. What does this tell us about our relationship with our employer?

_____

_____

_____

_____

3. Balancing one's job and family responsibilities is often a severe problem. What specific things can a man do to bring these two elements into balance?

_____

_____

_____

4. If your boss asked you to do something unethical, and you knew that not to do it would put your job in jeopardy, what would you do? Why?

_____

_____

_____

_____

_____

5. In what ways can you glorify God by the work that you do?

_____

_____

_____

_____

_____

6. How can you better support your wife when your job requires you to travel or to work overtime to finish a project? If your wife is a stay-at-home mother with small children, how can you support the work that she does?

_____

_____

_____

_____

_____

_____

7. Write a detailed description of what you would consider the perfect job. Why do you consider it perfect, and how do you think God would judge it, based on today's lesson?

_____

_____

_____

_____

_____

Action Plan:

This week I will try to be more faithful to my family and my job by:
- ● evaluating the priorities and goals in my life.
- ● discussing with my spouse how my job impacts the quality of our family life.
- ● evaluating the reasons I spend as much time on the job as I do.
- ● other:

_____

_____

Lesson 42

Building Relationships

1 Samuel 18:1-5; Sirach 6:5-17; John 15:12-17; Ecclesiastes 4:9-10
Catechism: 609; 1970-1972

One of the most remarkable friendships in all of history was between David and Jonathan, the son of King Saul, who would inherit the throne. Against his own self-interest and the desires of his father, he became a friend and supporter of David. He gave David his own armor and made a covenant with him, because "he loved him as himself."

When Saul was bent on killing David, Jonathan interceded and reconciled, at least temporarily, his father and his friend. When Saul's anger against David rose up again, Jonathan recommitted his allegiance to David, saying, "I will do whatever you wish" (1 Samuel 20:4). Ultimately, he and David entered into a sacred covenant, swearing to each other that: "The LORD shall be between you and me forever" (1 Samuel 20:23).

Jonathan and Saul were both killed in battle. There is a beautiful passage in 2 Samuel 1:26 in which David prays over their bodies: "I grieve for you, Jonathan my brother! /most dear have you been to me; /More precious have I held love for you /than love for women."

1. The greatest obstacles to deep friendships between men are:

_____
_____
_____
_____
_____

2. List the characteristics of an ideal Christian friendship. Why are these characteristics important to you?

_____
_____
_____
_____
_____

3. Identify some of the ways friendships between men can be an aid to living a fully Christian life. How can they be detrimental?

_____
_____
_____
_____
_____

4. Identify the one quality you would most want in a close friend. Explain your answer.

_____

_____

_____

_____

_____

5. Jesus laid down his life for his friends. How is God calling you to lay down your life for your friends?

_____

_____

_____

_____

_____

6. Several of the Catechism and scripture references in this lesson speak of the need for love. How can a man appropriately show love for another man?

_____

_____

_____

_____

_____

7. List the male friends whom you would go to for advice or encouragement on a critical life issue. Why would you choose these men?

_____

_____

_____

_____

_____

Action Plan:

Over the next week I will take stock of my relationships with other men by:
- identifying the positive elements I take to the relationships.
- identifying and working to eliminate the negative elements I take to the relationships.
- resolving to do one thing this week that will strengthen my relationship with my best male friend.
- other:

_____

_____

_____

Lesson 43

Shooting Straight

Speaking the Truth in Love

John 14:6; James 5:19-20; 2 Timothy 2:22-26
Catechism: 2467-2470; 2478

Jim called Dave to say he was stopping by his office on the way home. Dave, a lawyer, had been neglecting his law practice to help develop a Christian ministry for men. Dave had a wife and young children who were also being neglected because of the ministry. Jim arrived at the office and sat down across the conference room table from Dave and said, "Dave, you know I've always spoken straight with you, and it's always been out of love. So here goes: You're screwing up! You need to get your priorities straight and stop neglecting your practice and your family."

Jim's words were strong, and he was more than a little nervous. He wasn't sure whether his advice would cost him his friendship with Dave. Dave, for his part, listened to Jim respectfully. He realized that Jim had risked their friendship to tell him what he thought Dave needed to know. So, while Dave wasn't sure he totally agreed with what Jim was saying, he loved him for saying it. He was truly grateful to have such a friend.

1. Love and tenderness are necessary partners. Give some examples of situations in which the application of truth without love has led to negative consequences.

   _____
   _____
   _____
   _____
   _____

2. Give some examples of how compassion without truth has led to problems in our society.

   _____
   _____
   _____
   _____
   _____

3. Has anyone ever spoken the truth to you, lovingly and in your best interests? How did you respond?

   _____
   _____
   _____
   _____
   _____

4. Jesus said, "I am the way and the truth and the life" (John 14:6). Share a time in your life when your Christian values and beliefs helped you to confront a difficult or painful situation in your family or workplace.

_____

_____

_____

_____

_____

5. Are there instances when it is better to withhold the truth from a person in order to protect them? How can you discern when to "speak the truth in love" and when not to?

_____

_____

_____

_____

_____

6. Your adult daughter is coming home to visit with her live-in boyfriend. She calls to confirm the time of their arrival and advises you that she and her boyfriend intend to share a room in your house. How do you respond?

_____

_____

_____

_____

_____

7. Truth is often said today to be relative, changing according to the circumstances. What truths guide your life? How do you defend them against those who say there are no absolutes?

_____

_____

_____

_____

_____

Action Plan:

This week I will reflect on how I speak the truth in love by:
- examining my motives when I have to speak a hard truth.
- stopping to consider the consequences of telling a "kind" lie.
- other:

_____

_____

_____

Lesson 44

Render unto Caesar

Christians and Civil Authority

Acts 5:25-29; Romans 13:1-7; 1 Peter 2:13-17
Catechism: 1897-1903, 2238-2240

Will left the office early with a touch of the winter flu. A fever and occasional chills made him feel terrible. All he could think about was getting home and going to bed. Little else caught his attention, including the fact that he was driving forty-five miles per hour in a thirty mile-per-hour zone, until he heard the siren. He looked into his rear view mirror, saw the flashing blue lights on the motorcycle, and realized he had been caught in a speed trap.

Will felt a mixture of emotions: embarrassment, anger, resentment. Responding to these emotions without thinking, Will decided, "When the cop comes up to my window to write a speeding ticket, I'll just breathe on him really hard and give him the flu. That'll serve him right."

1. Remember the last time you got a traffic ticket. How did you feel about the police officer who stopped you? What was wrong with Will's attitude? Was there anything wrong with yours?

   _____
   _____
   _____
   _____
   _____

2. As a child growing up, what authority figures did you most respect, and which ones did you find the hardest to respect?

   _____
   _____
   _____
   _____
   _____

3. Why do you think St. Paul told the Roman church not to resist civil authority?

   _____
   _____
   _____
   _____
   _____

4. The Catechism (2238) states that citizens should voice "just criticisms" of governments and laws when they seem harmful to human dignity and the good of the community. Share about a time when you voiced criticism of a civil law. Was it done constructively?

_____

_____

_____

_____

_____

5. How do you view the authority given to you in your job or in your family? Do you see it as handed down from God?

_____

_____

_____

_____

_____

_____

6. Describe a time when you were in conflict with authority. Was the authority "exercised legitimately"? (see Catechism 1903)

_____

_____

_____

_____

_____

_____

7. Describe how you think you would react if you suddenly learned that you were going to be imprisoned because of your religious beliefs. How do you think your family would feel?

_____

_____

_____

_____

_____

Action Plan:

This week I will examine my attitude toward civil authority by:
- ⦿ repenting of any ungodly attitudes about authority that are not justified.
- ⦿ identifying any areas where I might disagree with civil laws, such as the death penalty or abortion.
- ⦿ praying about what God is calling me to do to fight unjust laws.
- ⦿ other:

_____

_____

_____

As You Do unto the Least of These. . . .
Lesson 45

Social Action

Isaiah 58:5-11; Matthew 25:35-46; James 2:14-17
Catechism: 1929; 1939-1940; 2447

Tim had always been generous in contributing to charitable causes, but he had never given much thought to the disparity in wealth between rich and poor countries. A job promotion, however, gave him the chance to travel to a third world country. The abject poverty of the people he saw there astounded him. He had no idea people could have so little. The trip transformed Tim. From having a passing concern for the poor, Tim now immersed himself in the teachings of the church on social justice. His interest led him to become involved in an international organization that helped poor people start small businesses of their own. Several times, Tim even traveled to third world countries on the organization's behalf. Tim knew his efforts were a drop in the bucket compared to the needs of people everywhere. Still, every time he met someone who had been helped by the work of the group, he was filled with joy and gratitude for the privilege God had given him to serve the least of his brothers.

1. In his encyclical on social justice, Pope John Paul II called on all Catholics to stand in solidarity with the poor and the oppressed—not just to help them, but to be one of them. Give some real life examples of how this can be done.

   _____
   _____
   _____
   _____
   _____

2. What is your parish doing to stand in solidarity with the poor?

   _____
   _____
   _____
   _____
   _____

3. How do you determine how much of the world's goods are sufficient for your family?

   _____
   _____
   _____
   _____
   _____

4. You are leaving church after a Mass during which the pastor gave an impassioned homily on responding to the needs of the poor. Your friend nudges you and says, "I wish Father would stick to religion and stay out of politics." How do you respond?

_____

_____

_____

_____

_____

5. If you were to analyze your daily calendar and your checkbook, what would the analysis say about your priorities in relation to the poor and less affluent?

_____

_____

_____

_____

_____

6. What have you done to lead your wife and children in the area of the family's social responsibility?

_____

_____

_____

_____

_____

7. Jesus said he came to serve, not to be served (Matthew 20:28). Where do you stand in imitating this Christ-like servant mentality? Be specific.

_____

_____

_____

_____

Action Plan:

I will try to stand in solidarity with the poor as the Church teaches by:
- making myself more aware of the social teachings of the Church.
- paying more attention to the plight of the invisible poor and oppressed in my environment.
- praying about giving of my time and money to a charity or ministry which serves the downtrodden.
- other:

_____

_____

Some of My Best Friends Are. . .
Lesson 46

Prejudice

Luke 19:1-10; Galatians 3:26-29
Catechism: 1934-1935; 2412

Sam and his friend Mike were at a college football game. They were seated behind some people who were obviously not from the city. As the game progressed, the people in front of Sam and Mike became louder and louder as they cheered for their team. Their language, even though it was not profane, showed a lack of education.

After the game as they were walking to the car, Sam said, "Those guys sitting in front of us were sure a bunch of hicks. You wonder why people like that don't do something about their ignorance." At first, Mike kept silent, but Sam could see by the look on his face that Mike was uncomfortable with his remark. "What's the matter?" Sam asked. "It just sounds as if you have a prejudice against people who aren't as sophisticated or as educated as you are," Mike replied. Sam was upset at the accusation. He prided himself on his lack of prejudice. Later, though, he realized that Mike was probably right. Sam had always thought of prejudice in terms of race, but maybe prejudice could apply to social class as well.

1. When we think of prejudice, we most often think of racial prejudice. What other kinds of prejudice have you observed?

   _____

   _____

   _____

   _____

   _____

2. Tell of a time when you personally experienced or observed prejudice. How did you react? How did you feel?

   _____

   _____

   _____

   _____

   _____

3. The Second Vatican Council said that any type of discrimination is "incompatible with God's design" (see Catechism 1935). What is the basis for this truth?

   _____

   _____

   _____

   _____

4. If Jesus had prejudged Zacchaeus (Luke 19:1-10), he would have missed an opportunity to lead him to salvation. Has there ever been a time when prejudice kept you from leading another to Christ?

_____

_____

_____

_____

5. Paragraph 2412 of the Catechism says, "Reparation for injustice committed requires the restitution of stolen goods to their owner." How does the injustice of prejudice steal from the victim, and how can one practically make restitution?

_____

_____

_____

_____

_____

6. Prejudice is often difficult to see in oneself because of the acceptance of societal norms. Discuss any prejudices that you think are generally accepted in our society.

_____

_____

_____

_____

_____

7. Discuss with your group the root causes of prejudice, and why you think prejudice continues to be so prevalent in our society today.

_____

_____

_____

Action Plan:

I will work at being more aware of prejudice in my world this week by:
- looking for any form of prejudice in my life toward others.
- identifying a form of prejudice in my environment that is generally accepted, and doing something about it.
- getting to know someone from a different racial, religious, or social group.
- praying daily to be strong in avoiding temptations.
- other:

_____

_____

_____

Lesson 47

Am I My Brother's Keeper?

Caring for the Needs of Others

Genesis 4:1-10; 2 Samuel 12:1-8; Luke 10:25-37

Catechism: 1878-1879, 2448

Jeff and Roger had known each other for a number of years. Although they were not close friends, they sometimes played golf together and discussed various aspects of their lives, including their work. On one occasion, Jeff confided in Roger that a very attractive female executive in his company had been coming on to him. In the process she had intimated that if he would help her do some business things that were ethically questionable, there could be some attractive rewards for him.

Roger's initial response was to just listen and keep his nose out of Jeff's business. After all, Jeff had not asked him for advice. Then he remembered the story of Cain and Abel and he thought to himself, "Am I my brother's keeper?"

1. Share with the group a situation in which you were faced with a decision to be your "brother's keeper." How did you respond? Why? What were your feelings?

_____

_____

_____

_____

2. What are the consequences of being your brother's keeper, or refusing to be?

_____

_____

_____

_____

_____

3. Describe a time when someone tried to look out for you. What were your feelings? How did you respond?

_____

_____

_____

_____

4. Has envy, or any other sin, ever prevented you from reaching out to a brother?

_____

_____

_____

_____

_____

5. What organizations in your community seek to care for the needs, both physical and spiritual, of others? How can you best support these organizations?

_____

_____

_____

_____

_____

_____

6. What should be the attitudes of employers in taking care of the needs of their employees? In your profession, how do you, or how do you not, practice being your brother's keeper?

_____

_____

_____

_____

_____

_____

7. The Catholic Church has expressed "a preferential love" for the poor (see Catechism 2448). How does this relate to being our brother's keeper in third world countries?

_____

_____

_____

_____

_____

_____

Action Plan:

Out of love for my brothers, I will:
- try to make a friend, be a friend, and bring a friend to Christ.
- be more open to the needs of my brothers.
- resist the tendency to not get involved.
- other:

_____

_____

_____

Where Have All the Heroes Gone?
Lesson 48

Heroes/Role Models

1 Samuel 17:51b; Proverbs 27:17

Catechism: 1803-1804

Kevin was a committed Catholic college student who was asked by his pastor to become active in the parish youth ministry. It didn't take long for the teens in the youth group to become attached to Kevin. They liked his sense of humor and warmth. They were impressed by his athletic abilities. But mostly they were amazed at his love for God. They had never met such a "cool" college student who talked about his desire to pray and serve the church. Their "heroes" had always been rock stars and sports figures who often glorified immorality and selfishness. Kevin was someone they could admire and emulate. Kevin realized that he had become a role model for the kids, and he thanked the Lord for the privilege to serve in his parish. He also realized that God had given him a great responsibility to influence the lives of these teens. Kevin knew he would have to stay close to God and the Church in order to fulfill that responsibility.

1. Why was Goliath a hero to the Philistines? What qualities usually make a person a "hero" to others?

   _____

   _____

   _____

   _____

   _____

2. Who are some positive Biblical role models? What virtues did these individuals exhibit?

   _____

   _____

   _____

   _____

   _____

3. Describe a positive role model in your life. What effect did this individual have on you? Be specific.

   _____

   _____

   _____

   _____

   _____

4. Describe a situation in which you served as a hero or positive role model for another. What difference did you make in this person's life?

_____
_____
_____
_____
_____

5. How would you explain the statement in Proverbs 27:17?

_____
_____
_____
_____
_____

6. Jesus is the ultimate role model for living a Christian life. From your personal experience and your observation of others, how well are you responding to his example? Explain your answer.

_____
_____
_____
_____
_____

7. Name one individual from the last one hundred years whom you would identify as today's most positive hero and Christian role model. What virtues did this person exhibit?

_____
_____
_____
_____

Action Plan:

I will try to be a better role model for others by:
◉ praying for guidance in my life.
◉ being more aware of the consequences of my behavior on others.
◉ seeking a positive role model for myself.
◉ other:

_____
_____
_____

Lesson 49

The Household of God

Building Up the Body of Christ

Romans 9:1-6; Ephesians 4:1-16

Catechism: 813; 845; 865

St. Paul makes an extraordinary statement in chapter nine of his Letter to the Romans. He knows that many of the Jews are rejecting the teachings about Jesus. Rather than become angry and frustrated, Paul says that he has "great sorrow and constant anguish in my heart." He goes on to say that he almost wishes he were "accursed and separated from Christ" for the sake of his brothers (9:2-3).

Paul is saying, in so many words, that if we can't all go to Jesus together, what's the point of going? He feels such a oneness with his kinsmen, the Jewish people, that it's hard for him to imagine salvation without them.

A fundamental principle of Christianity, but one which many have trouble understanding, is that the Body of Christ is constantly being built up, unified, and moving toward perfection. In a sense, we all go together. This is such a mystery, but we must live our lives based upon this principle. We must live now with the conscious thought at all times that we will do all we can to unify the Body of Christ and promote its growth.

1. There are those who would say they don't need the Church to be a good Christian and to receive salvation. How would you respond to such a person?

2. In many parishes there exist factions, divided on issues from interpretation of doctrine to the color of carpet. Why is unity so vital for the Church?

3. What are some of the obstacles to a sense of unity in the Body of Christ?

4. What gifts has God given you with which to build up his Body, and how effectively are you using them?

_____

_____

_____

_____

5. Of the five gifts mentioned in Ephesians 4:2, which one most needs to be developed in your life?

_____

_____

_____

_____

_____

6. What practical things happen in your parish that build up the Body of Christ?

_____

_____

_____

_____

_____

7. St. Paul told the Corinthians, "If [one] part suffers, all the parts suffer with it; if one part is honored, all the parts share its joy" (1 Corinthians 12:26). How do we share in the suffering and joy of another? How does this build up the Body of Christ?

_____

_____

_____

_____

_____

Action Plan:

I will try to be more aware of my responsibility to build up the Body of Christ by:
- examining my gifts and how I am using them.
- seeking unity if I am involved in a faction in my parish.
- other:

_____

_____

Lesson 50

That They Be One

Protestant Brothers

Mark 9:38-42; John 17:20-21; Ephesians 4:1-6
Catechism: 817-822; 847

Hector and Phil were next-door neighbors and close friends. One day, Hector and his family were over for a backyard barbecue with some families from Phil's church. The conversation turned to a discussion of an upcoming Promise Keepers stadium gathering in a nearby city. More than 60,000 men were expected to attend. The men invited Hector, a Catholic, to go with them. Hector had heard of Promise Keepers, but didn't know much about them. He went to a fellow parishioner for advice about participating with his neighbor and friends and was told that he shouldn't go to the event, "because Catholics shouldn't get involved in those Protestant things." This left Hector confused.

1. If you were Hector, how would you respond to the situation described above?

_____

_____

_____

_____

_____

2. Have you ever participated in an ecumenical religious event? What was your experience?

_____

_____

_____

_____

_____

3. What should be our attitude toward our Protestant brothers who are sincerely committed to their religious beliefs?

_____

_____

_____

_____

_____

4. In your own lifetime, how have you seen unity advance among Christians of various denominations? Where do you see room for more progress?

_____

_____

_____

_____

_____

5. What are some of the ways we can respond with our Protestant brothers to Jesus' call for unity? Is your parish involved in any of these?

_____

_____

_____

_____

_____

6. It has been estimated that there are some 26,000 religious sects that claim to be Christian. What statement does this make to people from non-Christian religions?

_____

_____

_____

_____

_____

7. Regarding Christian unity, what is the difference between uniformity and unity?

_____

_____

_____

_____

Action Plan:

In response to Jesus' prayer for unity, I will:
- ◉ study to better understand what is meant by Christian unity.
- ◉ share my faith story with a Protestant friend and listen to his.
- ◉ pray for unity.
- ◉ other:

_____

_____

_____

_____

Lesson 51

Go and Make Disciples

Evangelization

Matthew 28:18-20; Luke 4:43; Acts 1:8; 1 Corinthians 9:16
Catechism: 730; 849

Wayne and Charlie were having their weekly lunch together. Charlie, a recent convert to a non-denominational faith, was bubbling over with excitement about a new program at his church. All of the members of his congregation were in a training program to learn how to evangelize. Charlie told Wayne about how he had been helped to put his faith story into words, and how he had been taught to defend his faith with passages from the Bible. Every member of the church was being urged to go out and witness to Jesus Christ to all of their friends and families.

Wayne, a life-long Catholic, found all of this very strange. He thought to himself, "That's why we have priests, deacons and religious." The next weekend, he mentioned the activities over at Charlie's church to his pastor. The pastor didn't have too much to say in answer to Wayne's questions. Instead he suggested that Wayne read *On Evangelization in the Modern World*, by Pope Paul VI, and *Go and Make Disciples*, a document published by the bishops of the United States.

1. From your personal experience, how do Catholics react to the word *evangelization*? What is your reaction?

_____
_____
_____
_____
_____

2. Pope Paul VI in *On Evangelization in the Modern World*, said "She [the Church] exists in order to evangelize." How would you describe Catholic evangelization?

_____
_____
_____
_____
_____

3. What are the implications for you personally of Luke 4:43, read in light of paragraphs 730 and 849 of the Catechism?

_____
_____
_____
_____
_____

4. St. Paul speaks of being obligated to preach the gospel. Do you feel this same obligation? Explain your answer, including how you can do this as a lay person.

_____

_____

_____

_____

_____

5. List and discuss the things your parish is doing in response to the Great Commission of Matthew 28:19.

_____

_____

_____

_____

_____

6. Discuss the dimensions of social outreach and community presented in the Great Commission. How is the Great Commission more than just preaching?

_____

_____

_____

_____

_____

7. How do you proclaim Christ as number one in your life?

_____

_____

_____

_____

_____

Action Plan:

I will seek to become a better evangelizer by:

- reading *On Evangelization in the Modern World* or the U.S. Bishops' *Go and Make Disciples*.
- becoming involved in one of the evangelizing ministries of my parish.
- speaking to my pastor about establishing an evangelization committee, if one does not exist in my parish.
- befriending one of my unchurched neighbors, praying for him, and asking God for opportunities to share my faith story with him.
- other:

_____

_____

_____

Lesson 52

Looking Back, Looking Forward

Psalms 37:3-7,18,23-34; Proverbs 16:1-9,20

Catechism: 1914

It was New Year's Eve. Joe and Harry were chatting, waiting for the office to close so they could begin their year-end celebrations. Joe commented to Harry, "You know, I don't know where the year went. It seemed to go so fast that I didn't do very much of what I resolved to do at the beginning of the year. It seems like I had to deal with the same old problems and challenges that I struggled with the year before. Nothing seems to change. Well, so much for New Year's resolutions." Harry replied, "I'm not big on New Year's resolutions, but I do try to start off every year with some goals in mind. I didn't meet all the goals I set for myself and my family this year, but I did make some progress. This year we started praying as a family more often. Next year I'd like to see if we can pray together every day." As he drove home that day, Joe thought about what Harry had said and felt more hopeful. Maybe he and his wife could pray and talk about some goals for the new year.

1. Why do you think Joe was unable to move forward in the year that had just passed?

_____

_____

_____

_____

_____

2. How would things have changed if Joe had prayed before the year had started about what God wanted him to do that year?

_____

_____

_____

_____

3. Of the areas in your life where you struggled in the past year, how was God guiding you? Did you feel that the Lord was with you each step of the way, or that you were going it alone?

_____

_____

_____

_____

_____

4. Most of us make New Year's resolutions. Do you also develop a plan to help you keep those resolutions? If so, share that plan with your group.

_____

_____

_____

_____

_____

5. In Proverbs 16, we are told that God helps us in our planning. How do you experience God's help and direction in your own planning?

_____

_____

_____

_____

_____

6. What areas of your life would you like to be different in the new year? What kind of a plan do you need to make this happen?

_____

_____

_____

_____

_____

7. What one thing can you do to assure that you will learn from past mistakes and move in the direction you want to go in the new year?

_____

_____

_____

_____

_____

Action Plan:

I will try to improve myself and my environment by:
- praying for the Lord to guide me in the coming year.
- developing meaningful and specific resolutions for the new year.
- developing a workable plan to implement my resolutions.
- stopping periodically to reflect on how well my plan is working.
- frequently questioning if my plans are in accordance with God's plans.
- other:

_____

_____

Other Resources From The Word Among Us Press

The Wisdom Series:

Hold Fast to God: Wisdom from The Early Church

A Radical Love: Wisdom from Dorothy Day

Welcoming the New Millennium:
   Wisdom from Pope John Paul II

My Heart Speaks: Wisdom from Pope John XXIII

Live Jesus! Wisdom from Saints Francis de Sales
   and Jane de Chantal

Love Songs: Wisdom from St. Bernard of Clairvaux

Walking with the Father: Wisdom from Brother Lawrence

Touching the Risen Christ: Wisdom from the Fathers

These popular books include short biographies of the authors and selections from their writings grouped around themes such as prayer, forgiveness, and mercy.

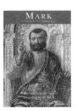

The New Testament Devotional Commentary Series:

Matthew: A Devotional Commentary

Mark: A Devotional Commentary

Luke: A Devotional Commentary

John: A Devotional Commentary

Acts of the Apostles: A Devotional Commentary

Leo Zanchettin, General Editor

Practical commentaries that include each passage of Scripture with a faith-filled meditation. These commentaries draw from solid Catholic scholarship as well as inspire readers to grow in their love for Christ. Readers will find new and rich meanings as they meet Jesus through the eyes of the New Testament writers.

Books on Saints:

A Great Cloud of Witnesses: The Stories of 16 Saints and Christian Heroes by Leo Zanchettin and Patricia Mitchell

I Have Called You by Name: The Stories of 16 Saints and Christian Heroes by Patricia Mitchell

Each book contains inspiring biographies, along with selections of the saints' own writings.

To order call 1-800-775-9673
www.wau.org